Wonderful Words, Silent Truth

Poets on Poetry   Donald Hall, General Editor

Charles Simic

Wonderful Words, Silent Truth

ESSAYS ON POETRY AND A MEMOIR

Ann Arbor
The University of Michigan Press

Copyright © by the University of Michigan 1990
All rights reserved
Published in the United States of America by
The University of Michigan Press
Manufactured in the United States of America

1993   1992   1991   1990   4   3   2

Library of Congress Cataloging-in-Publication Data

Simic, Charles, 1938–
    Wonderful words, silent truth : essays on poetry and a memoir /
Charles Simic.
        p.   cm.—(Poets on poetry)
    ISBN 0-472-09421-1.—ISBN 0-472-06421-5 (pbk.)
    1. Simic, Charles, 1938–   . 2. Poets, American—20th century—
Biography. 3. Poetry. I. Title. II. Series.
PS3569.I4725Z478   1990
814′.54—dc20   89-49606
                                                              CIP

For Nicky and Philip

Acknowledgments

Grateful acknowledgment is made to the following journals and publishers for permission to reprint previously published material.

Charioteer Press for "Introduction to the Poetry of Aleksandar Ristović," which first appeared in *Some Other Wine and Light* by Aleksandar Ristović. Copyright © 1989.

Denver Quarterly for "Visionaries and Anti-Visionaries," *Denver Quarterly* (Fall 1989).

Ecco Press for "Thomas Campion," which first appeared as the introduction to *The Essential Campion.* Copyright © 1988 by Charles Simic. First published by the Ecco Press in 1988, and reprinted by permission.

Field for "William Stafford's 'At the Bomb Testing Site,' " *Field* (Fall 1989).

Harper & Row for "At the Bomb Testing Site" from *New and Selected Poems* of William Stafford. Copyright © 1977 by William Stafford. Reprinted by permission of Harper & Row.

Henry Holt and Company for "An Old Man's Winter Night" and "The Most of It" from *The Poetry of Robert Frost.* Copyright © 1975 by Lesley Frost Ballantine. Reprinted by permission of Henry Holt and Company, Inc.

Alfred A. Knopf, Inc., for "No Possum, No Sop, No Tatters," and "The Course of a Particular" from *The Palm at the End of the Mind* by Wallace Stevens. Copyright © 1971 by Holly Stevens. Reprinted by permission.

Little, Brown for "258" and "712" from *The Complete Poems of Emily Dickinson*. Copyright © 1960 by Mary L. Hampson. Reprinted by permission of Little, Brown.

New Literary History for "Notes on Poetry and Philosophy," *New Literary History* (Autumn 1989).

Quarry West for "Caballero Solo," *Quarry West* (1988).

Swallow Press/Ohio University Press for "Serbian Heroic Ballads," which first appeared as the preface to *The Battle of Kosovo*. Copyright © 1987.

Wesleyan University Press for "Ivan V. Lalić," which first appeared as the introduction to *Roll Call of Mirrors: Selected Poems of Ivan V. Lalić*. Copyright © 1988 by Charles Simic. Reprinted by permission of Wesleyan University Press.

Every effort has been made to trace the ownership of all copyrighted material and to secure permission for its use.

Contents

Why I Like Certain Poems More
Than Others

I have a photograph of my father wearing a black tuxedo and holding a suckling pig under his arm. He's on stage. Two dark-eyed beauties in low-cut party dresses are standing next to him and giggling. He's laughing too. The pig has its mouth open, but it doesn't look as if it's laughing.

It's New Year's Eve. The year is 1926. They are in some kind of nightclub. At midnight the lights were turned off, and the pig was let go. In the pandemonium that ensued, my father caught the squealing animal. It was now his. After the bows, he got a rope from the waiter and tied the pig to the leg of their table.

He and the girls visited several other establishments that night. The pig went with them on a rope. They made it drink champagne and wear a party hat. "Poor pig," my father said years later.

At daybreak they were alone, the pig and my father, drinking in a low dive by the railroad station. At the next table a drunken priest was marrying a young couple. He crossed the knife and the fork to bless the newlyweds. My father gave them the pig as a wedding present. Poor pig.

That's not the end of the story, however. In 1948, when my father was already on his way to America and we were starving back in Belgrade, we used to barter our possessions for

---

Written in 1986 as an introduction to the issue of *Ploughshares* magazine which I edited.

food. You could get a chicken for a good pair of men's shoes. Our clocks, silverware, crystal vases, and fancy china were exchanged for bacon, lard, sausages, and such things. Once an old gypsy man wanted my father's top hat. It didn't even fit him. With that hat way down over his eyes, he handed over a live duck.

A few weeks later his brother came to see us. He looked prosperous. Gold teeth in front, two wristwatches, one on each hand. The other brother, it seems, had noticed a tuxedo we had. It was true. We let these people walk from room to room appraising the merchandise. They made themselves at home, opening drawers, peeking into closets. They knew we wouldn't object. We were very hungry.

Anyway, my mother brought out the 1926 tuxedo. We could see immediately the man was in love with it. He offered us first one, then two chickens for it. For some reason my mother got stubborn. The holidays were coming. She wanted a suckling pig. The gypsy got angry, or pretended to. A pig was too much. My mother, however, wouldn't give in. When she set her mind to it, she could really haggle. Years later in Dover, New Hampshire, I watched her drive a furniture salesman nuts. He offered to give her the couch for free just to get rid of her.

The gypsy was tougher. He marched out. Then, a few days later, he came back to take another look. He stood looking at the tux my mother had in the meantime brushed off. He looked and we looked. Finally, he let out a big sigh like a man making a difficult and irreversible decision. We got the pig the next day. It was alive and looked just like the one in the picture.

In the Beginning . . .

I

In the beginning . . . the radio. It sits on the table by my bed. It has a dial that lights up. The stations have names that then become visible. I can't read yet, but I make others read them to me. There's Oslo, Lisbon, Moscow, Berlin, Budapest, Monte Carlo, and still many more. One aligns the red arrow with a name and a strange language and unfamiliar music burst forth. At ten o'clock the stations sign off. The war is on. The year is 1943.

The nights of my childhood were spent in the company of that radio. I attribute my lifelong insomnia to its temptations. I couldn't keep my hands off it. Even after the stations went silent, I kept turning the dial and studying the various noises. Once I heard beeps in Morse code. Spies, I thought. At times I'd catch a distant station so faint I'd have to turn the sound all the way up and press my ear against the rough burlap that covered the speaker. Somewhere dance music was playing or the language was so appealing I'd listen to it for a long time, feeling myself on the verge of understanding.

All this was strictly forbidden. I was supposed to be asleep. Come to think of it, I must have been afraid to be alone in that big room. The war was on. The country was occupied. Terrible things happened at night. There was a curfew. Someone

This autobiographical piece was first written for volume 4 of the Contemporary Authors, Autobiography Series published by Gale Research and appeared there and in *Antaeus.* The present version is revised and much expanded.

was late. Someone else was pacing up and down in the next room. Black paper curtains hung over the windows. It was dangerous even to peek between them at the street—the dark and empty street.

I see myself on tiptoes, one hand on the curtain, wanting to look but afraid of the light the radio tubes cast dimly through its trellised back onto the bedroom wall. My father is late and outside the roofs are covered with snow.

The Germans bombed Belgrade in April of 1941, when I was three years old. The building across the street was hit and destroyed. I don't remember anything about that bomb, although I was told later that I was thrown out of my bed and across the room when it hit. The next day we left the city on foot. I remember a beautiful meadow, great clouds overhead, and then suddenly a plane flying very low.

Did we leap into a ditch by the railroad tracks, or was that some other time? How many of us were there? I remember my mother but not my father. There were people I didn't know, too. I see their hunched backs, see them running with their bundles, but no faces . . . My film keeps breaking. An image here and there, but not much continuity. And the lighting is poor. I have to strain my eyes as the light gets dimmer and dimmer.

Was the world really so gray then? In my early memories, it's almost always late fall. The soldiers are gray and so are the people.

The Germans are standing on the street corner. We are walking by. "Don't look at them," my mother whispers. I look anyway, and one of them smiles. For some reason that makes me afraid.

One night the Gestapo came to arrest my father. This time I was asleep and awoke suddenly to the bright lights. They were rummaging everywhere and making a lot of noise. My father was already dressed. He was saying something, probably cracking a joke. That was his style. No matter how bleak the situation, he'd find something funny to say. Years later, surrounded by doctors and nurses after having suffered a bad heart attack, he replied to their "how're you feeling sir" with a request for some pizza and beer. The doctors thought he had suffered brain damage. I had to tell them that this was normal behavior for him.

I guess I went to sleep after they took him away. In any case, nothing much happened this time. He was released. It wasn't his fault his kid brother stole a German army truck to take his girlfriend for a spin. He didn't even get shot—that brother of his! The Germans were astonished, almost amused by his stupidity. They shipped him off to work in Germany. They made the attempt, that is, but he slipped through their fingers.

In the meantime, my friends and I were playing war. All the kids were playing war. We took prisoners. We fell down dead. We machine-gunned a lot. Rat-tat-tat! How we loved the sound of machine guns.

This kind of playing drove the grown-ups crazy. There was already so much real shooting in the world, and now these kids with their imaginary guns! It didn't take much to make them fly off the handle. They'd look so preoccupied, and then all of a sudden—pop! You'd see a woman stop in the middle of the street and slap her child, seemingly for no reason at all, and with everybody watching.

You couldn't blame them, really. I had a friend, for example, who could imitate an air-raid siren perfectly. Every time his parents left him at home alone, he'd stand on their sixth-floor balcony and wail. People on the street would threaten him first, then plead with him to stop. He wouldn't. Instead, he'd get even louder, even more inspired. We thought it was all very funny.

The building we lived in was in the very center of the city on a small side street near the main post office and parliament. A dangerous place to be. That's what we realized in the spring of 1944 when the English and the Americans started bombing Belgrade.

It was Easter Sunday (a nice day to pick for a bombing raid). The dining-room table was already set in a festive way with our best china when the planes came. We could hear them. The windows were open, since it was such a beautiful spring day.

"The Americans are throwing Easter eggs," my father said. Then, it started thundering. We ran down to the cellar. The building shook. People huddled on the floor. One could hear glass breaking up above. Some kid ran to the stairs to take a look. His mother screamed.

Then it was all over. We crawled out. The street was dark. All the dust of the city had risen in the air. A man covered with fallen plaster walked by telling everybody that a certain neighborhood had been leveled. That was astonishing. It was one of the poorest neighborhoods in the city. There were no Germans there.

The next day the Allies came again and it was the same. They never hit anything of military importance. A bomb landed on our sidewalk. It didn't explode. My mother was all for leaving immediately; my father was for staying. She prevailed.

The roads out of the city were full of refugees. The planes kept returning. We approved of the American and the English bombing of the Germans. I never heard anyone complain. They were our allies. We loved them. Still, with their miserable marksmanship, it was dangerous to remain in the city.

My grandfather had a summer house not far from Belgrade. When we arrived there, my father's side of the family had already assembled. They argued all the time. In addition to the German occupation, a civil war was going on in Yugoslavia. There were at least half-a-dozen factions made up of Royalists, Communists, Fascists, and various other collaborators, all slaughtering each other. Our family was bitterly divided between the Royalists and the Communists. My grandfather remained neutral. They were all the same in his opinion.

As for my mother, she said nothing. She disliked my father's people. She came from an old middle-class family, while they were blue-collar workers. She was educated in Paris, while they sat around getting drunk in taverns. That's how she saw it. It's astonishing that she and my father ever got together. My father had gone to the university and was now a successful engineer, but he had an equally low opinion of my mother's world.

It wasn't long before he left us. Early one morning my mother and I accompanied him to the small and crowded train station. By the way he looked at us, and by the way he hugged me, I knew this was no ordinary journey. I was told nothing. Ten years would pass before I would see him again. People would ask, "Where's your father?" and I couldn't tell them. All my mother knew that day was that he was attempting to get to Italy, but there was no news of him for a long time.

We stayed with my grandparents. Summer came. The bombing of Belgrade continued. We could see the planes high over the city. Our house was on a hill overlooking the river Sava and had a fine view in that direction. Columns of smoke went up as the bombs fell. We'd be eating watermelon in our garden, making pigs of ourselves while watching the city burn. My grandmother would cross herself repeatedly. The dogs would get restless.

The garden was overgrown with tall sunflowers and weeds. I'd go hide among them, except there were rattlesnakes everywhere, including the rockpile under my window. I'd sit on the steps talking to them, while they hissed back. Once I threw a stone at one, missed, and worried it would come that night and visit me in my bed.

I slept and went around naked. It was so hot. The river was close by but we only went to dip our feet. There were corpses in it. Every few days they'd fish one out. Some people didn't care. One evening I saw some young women splashing under the willows in their slips, but when I drew close to take a better look, I saw a couple of armed men sitting in the shadows and smoking. Their beaus I presumed.

That time I was alone for some reason. Mostly I was not allowed to wander around. The world was full of bad people. A boy my age who lived across the street was attacked by a man who kept biting him on the neck. It happened in broad daylight as he was standing in front of his house.

For days on end I did nothing but stay in my room playing. I remember lying on the floor eye to eye with one of my toy soldiers, or watching flies walk across the ceiling. Except for these few scattered images, I have no idea what I thought, what I felt.

One night a munitions factory several miles away blew up. Again I was thrown out of bed. The room was lit up. Night had turned into day. We sat up till dawn watching the fiery sky. In the morning there was a big movement of troops. They went around confiscating the few domestic animals that were still around. Afterwards, you could not hear a hen cackle, a rooster crow anywhere.

The fighting was intensifying. The Russian Army was in southern Rumania pushing toward Belgrade along the Danube. Locally, the various political and guerrilla factions were settling scores. There was a lot of indiscriminate killing. After I found some bodies in the roadside ditch near our house, I was not allowed to go out anymore. Our neighbors were executed in their own home. The people across the street just disappeared. Nothing happened to us. My mother was very pregnant and wobbled around. She had no politics, and neither did my grandfather. That doesn't explain it, of course. We were just lucky, I guess.

It was a relief when the Russians finally came. At least now there were only two sides fighting. The Germans had retreated across the river from us. One could see them go about their business, bringing up some artillery pieces. The Russians had their own guns just above our house. It was clear, if both sides started shooting, we'd be right in the middle.

Pregnant as she was, my mother decided to flee to a village further up beyond the hill where we knew some people. My grandparents retreated to the cellar.

It was mid-October 1944. The road to the village was empty and so was the farmhouse of our friend, where we found only a very old woman who gave us some goat's milk. That whole day we sat in the kitchen with that silent old woman and waited for the people to come back. I remember the chill, the gray light in the window, and how my mother kept reminding me to keep quiet.

Toward dusk we heard steps. A wild-looking man with blood on his face told us, without even stopping, that the

Germans were coming this way and killing everybody in sight. There was nothing else to do but hurry back to the grandfather's house. The old woman stayed behind. We were back on that empty road lined with poplars. It was so quiet we could hear our quick steps. All of a sudden there were shots. A bullet whizzed by. My mother pulled me to the ground and threw herself over me. Then it was quiet again. Just our hearts beating. No more shots.

After a long, long time, we raised our heads. It had cleared up. The sky was cloudless. The first few evening stars were in their places. We rose slowly and stood for a while in the deep shadow of the trees. Then we resumed our way under cover of darkness. When we got back, my grandfather was sitting at the table, drinking a toast with a Russian officer and grinning at us.

My wartime adventures really began the day the Russians liberated Belgrade. We had gotten back to our apartment through the rubble of fighting and celebrating crowds, since my mother wanted to be near her doctor. The very next day she managed somehow to get herself a cot in the basement of a private clinic in order to await the termination of her pregnancy. As it turned out, she stayed there a month. I was entrusted to the care of one of my mother's aunts, the only relative we had left in the city.

Nana was the black sheep in the family. It was whispered that she cheated on her old husband, was spending his money recklessly, and used bad language. That's what I loved about her. This elegant, good-looking woman would swear often and shamelessly.

I've no idea where Nana's husband was or why she was still in the city. I suspect she had her own private reasons. This was the second day of the liberation and there were still Germans holed up in our neighborhood, fighting. To my surprise she allowed me to go out on the street alone. There were other children out there, to be sure, but, still, this was strange. Often I'd return home and find no one. Later, I'd see her returning home, beautifully dressed, wearing gloves and high heels on the sidewalk strewn with broken glass and plaster. She'd be glad to see me and would have something special for me to eat, some unheard of delicacy like chocolate filled with nuts or smoked sausage.

Strangely enough she never went out at night. I've no memory of what we did in the evenings. Our building was almost empty. The lights were mostly out. There was nothing to do but sleep a lot. One morning, on awakening early, I saw my aunt washing her breasts in a pail of cold water. She caught me watching her and turned around. She burst out laughing and did a little dance, naked like that.

I was happy. My friends and I had plenty to do during the day and plenty of time to do it in. There was no school and our parents were either absent or busy. We roamed the neighborhood, climbed over the ruins, and watched the Russians and our partisans at work. There were still German snipers in a couple of places. We'd hear shots and take off running. There was a lot of military equipment lying around. The guns were gone, but there was other stuff. I got myself a German helmet. I wore empty ammo belts. I had a bayonet.

One day I was sitting with a friend in front of our building when a column of German prisoners came by escorted by some women soldiers. "Let's go and shoot some Germans, kids!" said one cheerily. Well, this was a bit too much. We said nothing. Actually, I doubt that we gave them a straight answer. One learned early to be circumspect and cautious. Never volunteer information, keep your mouth shut—that sort of thing. We followed them as far as the corner and then turned back. I remember one tall, blond German, straight as a broomstick. The others looked humpbacked in comparison.

Later, we went anyway. There was an old cemetery nearby with a huge church, and beyond it the fairgrounds, where supposedly, they were shooting German prisoners. We met a pack of children on the way who said that they were from the circus. It was true. There used to be a circus tent on the fairgrounds in the early years of the war, but now only a few trailers were left on its edge. These were odd-looking children. They wore the strangest clothes—unmatched, wrong-sized costumes—and they jabbered, speaking a foreign language among themselves.

"Show him what you can do," said my friend, who had met them before. They obliged. A little boy stood on his hands. Then, he removed one hand and was left for a moment standing on the other. A thin, dark-eyed, dark-haired girl leaned back until her head emerged from between her legs.

"They have no bones," my friend whispered. The dead have no bones, I thought. They fall over like sacks of flour.

The war went on. The Germans had dug in north of the city, on the other side of the rivers Sava and Danube. The Russians had left the fighting to the Yugoslavs while they advanced north toward Hungary. All able men were conscripted and the fighting was fierce. Belgrade was a city of the wounded. One saw people on crutches on every corner. They walked slowly, at times carrying a mess kit with their daily ration. There were soup kitchens where such people got their meals.

Once, chased by a friend, I rounded the corner of my street at top speed and collided with one of these invalids, spilling his soup on the sidewalk. I won't forget the look he gave me. "Oh child," he said softly. I was too stunned to speak. I didn't even have the sense to pick up his crutch. I watched him do it himself with great difficulty.

Around that time we heard that my mother's brother was wounded too. His story is absolutely incredible—as I found out later. He first fought with the Royalists, was captured by the Communists, lined up against the wall to be shot, and pardoned on the spot with the option that he join them. He did. The last few months of the war he fought with the Communists.

This is how he got wounded. He and two other soldiers were surrounded in a farmhouse by the Germans. They drew lots to see who would try to break out first. My uncle was last. The first man, after much hesitation, took off, only to be cut down by the Germans. The same thing happened to the second one, although he managed to run a good distance toward the woods. My uncle had no choice but to follow. At some point while running, he felt a great warmth. It was winter; the ground was covered with snow. Then he passed out.

When he came to, he was lying naked and barefoot in the farmhouse with most of his stuff stolen and a wound high up inside one of his thighs. He got up and stumbled out, shortly afterward reaching a road where eventually—it's hard for him to say how much time had elapsed—an old man came by in a horse cart, threw him a blanket, and took him along. All of a sudden—I still don't believe this—the old man was killed. A stray bullet hit him, and he fell over backwards where my uncle sat huddled. Luckily, the horses kept going, so eventually they reached some Russians, who took him to a medical unit where he was revived.

Now the tragic farce really begins. The Russians in those days had a cure-all for every serious leg wound: amputate the leg. That's what they told my uncle they were going to do. He was very unhappy, crying even, while the doctor cheerfully reminded him that he still had one leg left. Anyway, they strapped him to the field operating table and got ready to cut the leg, when all hell broke loose. Grenades, bombs flying. The tent collapsed. Everybody ran out, leaving him there. When the shooting was over, they came back but were no longer in the mood for the operation. He ended up, somehow, on a farm, where he was exceptionally well nursed by the kind people who lived there, and so on. End of that story.

By the time my brother was born, and he and my mother had come home from the clinic, I was in the business of selling gunpowder. It worked this way. Many of us kids had stashes of ammunition, which we had collected during the street fighting. The gunpowder from these rounds was sold to the older kids who, so I heard, were in turn selling it to the fishermen on the Danube. This last part I cannot guarantee. "Selling" is also the wrong word. We traded gunpowder for old comic books, toys, cans of food, and God-knows-what-else. I remember a particularly tasty can of American corned beef that I devoured all by myself, sitting in the winter sunlight behind the great Byzantine church of St. Mark.

I've no idea how long this went on. I had a large laundry

basket full of rounds of ammunition hidden in the cellar. Removing the gunpowder was done in the following way: one stuck the bullet part into the kitchen spigot and yanked the shell sideways until it came off. Absolute secrecy was, of course, required. My mother had no idea how I spent my time, although she was puzzled by some of the nice-looking toys I suddenly owned. But she was busy with the new baby and I was already an expert liar. Then, one day a kid on our block lost both of his hands. He was trying to remove the long black sticks of gunpowder from some sort of artillery shell. That's what he told me later while I tried to avoid looking at his two newly healed and still red stumps.

I started school in the spring of 1945, but I don't remember much about it. My parents taught me how to read early on, and I breezed through the first few grades. The classes that spring were sporadic. My interests, in any case, were elsewhere. The streets were full of semi-abandoned children. Gangs were being formed. Legendary hoods held whole neighborhoods in terror. One couldn't walk to school by the most direct route. There were enemies everywhere just waiting for someone like me to walk down their block.

We went in packs everywhere, but sometimes there was no choice. I had to go alone. I knew every backyard in my section of the city through which one could wind one's way unobserved. Still, a few times I got caught and beaten. For no reason. Just because I was from another neighborhood. The idea was not to cry, no matter how much it hurt, since seeing you cry made them happy. I know, because we did the same thing to the kids from other neighborhoods who were caught on our street.

When you're little you can't fight very well, so you'd better be quick on your feet. Luckily, I was—which was just as well, since someone was always trying to beat me up. An older boy in our neighborhood really had it in for me. This is what happened: He and a couple of other guys were going to the movies, and he had this can of beef—or whatever it was—which he wanted me to keep for him. No problem. I was happy to oblige. So they went off. A bit later the rest of us decided to play soccer on the street, so I decided to hide the can. I went into our building, made sure no one was following me, then descended toward the back where the entrance to the cellar was and where there was a pile of old furniture and some kind of large barrel in one of the corners, and placed the can of beef carefully behind the barrel. After again making sure that no one was watching me, I rejoined my friends on the street to play soccer.

Hours later, the owner of the can returned from the movies and asked me for it. I ran off to fetch it. When I got down there, when I reached behind that barrel in the dark, I discovered to my horror that the can wasn't there anymore. I couldn't believe it! It was impossible! I moved the furniture away from the wall, and even the heavy barrel, and still—nothing! A complete mystery, as I tried to tell its owner, who was waiting impatiently outside. He didn't believe me, of course. He started punching me right then and there while I protested my innocence.

As for the can, I never found out who swiped it and how. For years I'd think about it, visualizing every detail, remembering my caution and deliberateness, even down to the sound the can made as I placed it on the concrete floor. The best explanation is that one of my friends had followed me, but even if one did and was the culprit, he would have told me about it years later, since I brought the subject up often to everybody's amusement: The Mystery of Simic's Disappearing Can of American Army Beef. They all thought I had eaten it.

My mother had much to worry about. There was no news of my father. Unknown to us, he had reached Italy and was promptly arrested by the Germans, who accused him of being a spy. He was in prison in Milan for a few months when he was liberated by the Americans. He had no desire to return to Belgrade. He didn't like the Communists and he didn't get along with my mother. Before the war he had worked for an American company, had many American business connections, and had always wanted to see that country.

There were other reasons, too, for our concern. The Communists were firmly in power. People were being arrested left and right. Everybody was afraid. In school there was indoctrination.

I remember a young man coming to talk to us about Communism. The subject of religion came up. He said that there was no God and asked if some of us still believed in God. We all kept our mouths shut except for one scrawny little kid, who said he did. The fellow asked the kid what can God do? Everything, the kid said. Well, the fellow said, if you were to ask him to help you pick up this table, would he do it? I wouldn't ask him, said the kid, eyeing the heavy table. Why not? insisted the man. It'd be a dumb thing to ask for, replied the kid, barely audible.

That ended that. But there were more sinister things. One day the same young man asked if our parents at home complained about the new regime. No one said anything this time. When I told my mother what happened, she informed me, in no uncertain terms, that she would kill me if I ever opened my mouth. In any case, she did not take any chances. Anytime I walked into a room, the grown-ups would shut up and eye me suspiciously. I had plenty to be guilty about and it must have shown on my face, for there would be a long cross-examination: "What did you tell them?" "Nothing! I swear it!" And so it went.

My life on the street was also getting more complicated. I hung around with older boys. There was stealing. We stole for profit and for the fun of it—anything we could get our hands on that looked remotely valuable. I was usually the one to make the snatch, since I was the smallest and the fastest. I remember being chased by an ax-wielding man, whose bicycle pump I had taken from his yard while he had his back turned. I remember walking into a grocery store, grabbing something from the counter, and running away. This was for practice. There was not much to be found in those stores. Most of the food was rationed. If you took someone's monthly ration of sugar, you were committing an unforgivable crime.

Which reminds me. There were people who kept chickens and even pigs in their apartments if they could get them. I assume they were afraid to keep them in the backyard. They'd have to keep guard around the clock. There might have even been a law against it.

So, it was a secret. There'd be a rumor that so and so is keeping a pig in his bathroom. Supposedly, as the pig grew, they would give it the living room, and they themselves would move into the bathroom. That was the rumor anyway.

My mother was scandalized. The apartment on which the suspicion fell had previously belonged to a piano teacher. Now some hicks lived in it, but the piano was still there. My mother kept worrying about the piano, seeing the pig sleeping under it or scratching its back against one of the legs. Pretty funny, I thought.

But then it wasn't. When my friends heard about it, they figured we should steal the pig. I was supposed to climb on the third floor balcony when the people were at work, open the front door, and let the gang in and the pig out. Even more than the climb, the idea of meeting the pig terrified me. I imagined it to be huge. A monstrous hog with its hump reaching to the ceiling. Who knows what would have really happened if we had not gone on a trip just then.

My mother had heard that my father was alive and well in Trieste. She was determined that we should join him immediately. The frontier between Yugoslavia and Italy was still open, since the area around Trieste was disputed by the two countries. There was a chance we could slip across, but it was dangerous. One could get arrested. One could get shot, too, of course. My mother had no illusions about that. Still, she felt she had to try.

We left Belgrade for the coast in the fall of 1945. The train journey took forever. The tracks were still in terrible shape. All along the way one could see derailed trains and bombed-out stations. There were soldiers everywhere and tremendous crowds of people trying to get on the train. Although the Germans were gone, one could still feel their presence. We were Serbs in Croatian territory, and Croatian Fascists spent the war exterminating Serbs. We didn't open our mouths much.

This was the train my father took, I kept thinking. What I

was seeing now, he saw. That cluster of trees, for example. Or that house high on a hill! In Zagreb, we spent the night in a hotel. I remember the dark, poorly lit streets. They were empty. It was late. Our room was small and cold. Everything looked different. It was no longer the same country.

The next day, when we reached Opatia-Fiume, that once-fashionable Austro-Hungarian sea resort, we heard that the border was closed. Still, if one knew the right people, one could cross illegally. So we stayed.

It was a big, old seaside hotel with high, ornate ceilings, crystal chandeliers, and mirrors everywhere. We took our meals in a large, immaculately set and almost empty dining room, which looked out at the gray sea. I've wondered since who the few other guests were. They had a secretive air about them, didn't speak to each other, and rarely acknowledged our nods. I could walk for hours down the long hallways without meeting anyone or hearing a sound. Once I did hear sobs, muffled sobs, and even got my eye to the keyhole, but could see nothing. There was just the gray sea through the open balcony door and the silence of the hotel around me. The woman had stopped crying.

We went back to Belgrade, but my mother was stubborn. She found someone who knew a reliable person who, for a price, could take us across the border into Austria. I was told nothing. I was under the impression that we were going to spend our summer vacation in the mountains of Slovenia. Again, we found ourselves in an elegant, half-empty chalet, sleeping late and taking long mountain walks.

One evening, we walked farther than was our custom. We sat on a couple of rocks in the woods, and my mother told me that this was the night we'd be going to my father.

It was almost pitch dark when a man came to take us to a farmhouse where two armed men waited. The rest of the night we spent climbing the mountains, with my mother carrying my infant brother in her arms. They had given him something so he would sleep. We had to be absolutely quiet, even when we took brief rests.

We couldn't see much for most of the way. The moon only came out when we crossed the border in the wee hours. We were on the side of a hill, and Yugoslavia was down below. We sat on the grass and had our first talk of the night and the men smoked. This was a mistake, as it turned out. We heard someone shout something in German. One of our guides leapt to his feet and opened fire, and the two of them took off in the direction of Yugoslavia, leaving us alone. After a long while there was another shout in German. This time my mother replied, and soon enough they came out of the trees. We were in the hands of an American-Austrian border patrol, and that cheered us up tremendously.

The Americans took us to their barracks, where we spent the rest of the night. In the morning I had my first sight of the American army. Some of the soldiers were black, which fascinated me. Everybody was very friendly, giving us chewing gum and chocolate. We ate in the mess hall with everybody else, a big breakfast of eggs and bacon. There was even cocoa! My mother was happier than I've ever seen her. This was paradise.

Our problems started when the Americans handed us over to the English army, whose zone of occupation this was. A colonel sternly asked my mother for our passports. My mother laughed. After our all-night mountain hike our clothes were in tatters and our hands and faces were covered with scratches. My mother then tried a bit of humor. She told him, in the best English she could summon, that if we had had passports we would have surely taken a sleeping car. The fellow was not amused. All her explanations fell on deaf ears. What he did then—and it came to us as a big surprise and horror—is to drive us to the border and hand us over to the Yugoslav border guards. He saluted, they saluted, and we were back in Yugoslavia and under arrest.

We didn't know, of course, that this kind of thing happened often. The English were sending back Russian POW's and anybody else from Eastern Europe they got their hands on. People begged, threw their children off the trains, committed suicide. The English didn't care what happened. Their pal Stalin packed everybody off to the labor camps where, of course, many perished.

Our case was not so tragic. We were transported from prison to prison for the next two weeks, until we reached

Belgrade. Some of it was rather idyllic—like being escorted on foot through the gorgeous Slovenian countryside and stopping by some roadside orchard to eat apples together with our guard. At other times the cells were crowded, and there were some nasty-looking characters. I remember one tall old man who was supposed to have killed several people. He just stood in the middle of the cell, all day, with his eyes closed. Nobody dared come near him or speak above a whisper.

In Belgrade, my brother and I were released into the hands of my grandmother, and my mother was kept in prison for another four months. Her defense was that she simply wanted to be with her husband and was not given the legal means to do so. This was true enough, although probably not the reason why they let her go with so little fuss. The jails at that time were full of people with more interesting political transgressions. We were small fry. They slapped my mother a few times, once right in front of us, but that was all.

As for me, I thoroughly enjoyed being in jail. A couple of times they put me in with the men. This was hard on my mother because she worried that we'd get separated and she would not see me again. The cell doors would open at some ungodly night hour, when they take people to be interrogated, and this little kid would be pushed in. The prisoners were stunned. The cells were packed. They'd have to make room for me, make sure I had plenty of covers. They also wanted to hear my story. I obliged of course. The bedbugs made it hard to sleep. I embroidered, how I embroidered! I was at the center of attention. At home, too, all the relatives and friends were waiting to hear what happened. I reenacted the gunfight and the beatings of my mother for the benefit of all those grim and wary faces, night after night, inventing more and more fantastic details, until eventually they began to laugh at me and I stopped.

II

My childhood is a black and white movie. O rainy evenings, dimly lit streets! My mother leading me by the hand into the gloomy cinemas, where the performance has already started; where a boy is running down a country road under a sky full of ominous-looking clouds, where he kneels on someone's grave pulling weeds while the wind howls among the crosses and trees all around him; where later he visits a strange old woman, who sits in her wedding dress at the table full of moldy, cobweb-covered food. Mice run in and out of the huge wedding cake. Best of all there's a beautiful girl who teases him cruelly, whom he gets to kiss once on the dark staircase.

It's the dark ages I am describing now, things that happened forty years ago. My memory is so poor that everything looks badly lit and full of shadows. Even beautiful summer mornings lack the brightness they undoubtedly had. And the nights . . . they're as thick as the dreams from which one awakes troubled, yet unable to remember anything specific. Is that how it is with everybody?

Writing brings it back. There's the logic of chronology, which forces one to think about what comes next. There's also the logic of imagination. One image provokes another without rhyme or reason—perhaps with plenty of hidden rhyme and reason! I have to believe that. Otherwise, how do I explain why that movie scene has just reminded me of the great Hungarian hypnotist?

We had gone one night to see his show. It was in a big old hotel ballroom on Lake Bled in Slovenia. The place was packed, but also strangely silent. You know how it is with hypnotists, they are liable to call on you, bring you up on the stage and make you do strange things. This man had a reputation for doing wonders. And he looked the part: black clothes, black hair slicked down, bushy eyebrows, terrifying eyes, a commanding voice. He made my mother guess what was in people's pockets. She sat there on the stage with her eyes closed while he stood in the audience pointing at somebody. She spoke very slowly and in a kind of stage whisper. The audience gasped and then applauded.

I don't really remember this very well, though I will never forget how my mother's voice sounded. There was another person underneath the familiar one. A complete stranger I had to be wary of from now on.

The next morning in the hotel dining room we ended up sitting at the same table with the hypnotist during breakfast. It was simple. There were three of us, and he was alone, and there wasn't another empty chair in the place.

"Don't look at him," my mother whispered in my ear, kicking me under the table to emphasize the point. The hypnotist had no interest in us. I don't think he even recognized my mother from the night before. He ate his breakfast staring into his plate and chewing slowly. Even I could tell that he had false teeth. He was a very old man. When he held the butter knife, his hand trembled. We were done first, and left the table without looking back.

There was a time in 1947 or 1948 when we had almost nothing to eat. My mother didn't have her job at the conservatory back yet, and we had difficulty making ends meet. I remember coming from school one afternoon, telling her I was hungry, and watching her burst into tears. The only thing we had in the house that day were some onions, which I cut up. There was no oil, just some dry bread and salt. I remember thinking, this tastes pretty good.

My mother, who is an awful cook under any circumstances, used to make a kind of meatless stew, consisting of potatoes, onions, and perhaps a few carrots. This is what we ate all the time. By the third day, after all the reheating, the thing tasted foul. I'd gag with every mouthful and would have to drink big gulps of water in between to get it down. The bread was rationed. There would be only a large slice of black bread, which I always ate last, as a dessert.

The kids on the street talked about food all the time. Someone, for example, would describe a salami he had once had in great detail. We listened and asked questions about nuances of taste. Someone else spoke of the advantages and disadvantages of fried versus roasted chicken. Others liked sweets. They rhapsodized about ice cream, Swiss chocolate, various kinds of cakes and pies. My own contribution was almost always on the subject of pigs' ears. In my opinion, there was nothing tastier than roasted suckling pigs' ears. There was a story about that.

When the holidays came, everybody feasted. Belgrade is surrounded by farming country, and if one knew the right people one could get just about any kind of food—for a price. A fat peasant woman would come to see us on the sly, and after bargaining with my mother, would raise her skirts to reveal long strips of bacon wrapped around her waist.

Since we didn't have any money, we'd barter. A pair of my father's black patent leather dancing shoes went for a chicken. Sometimes these yokels couldn't make up their minds about what they wanted in exchange. We'd let them look around. They'd walk from room to room with us in tow, looking things over, shaking their heads when we suggested a particular item. They were hard to please. Carpets, clocks, armchairs, fancy vases were exchanged for various yard animals over the years.

Everybody did that. The sidewalks were covered with roasted suckling pigs on Christmas day. All sizes of pigs in all kinds of roasting pans. People brought them to the bakeries where, for a small charge, they'd be roasted in the big oven. By late morning there was no more room on the counters, so they had to put the pigs out until their owners came to collect them.

I remember the sight clearly, but I have no idea what year this was. It had started to snow, so one of the baker's helpers was trying to cover the roasted pigs with newspapers. The paper would get greasy immediately and wet. It was not easy to cover the pigs' ears. They were cocked, as if eavesdropping. A lot of people were milling around and jabbering while looking for their pans. Everybody was in a good mood. The pigs looked eager to be eaten.

Ours certainly did. I had to carry it several blocks over the slippery sidewalks. The pan was heavy. There was a lot of grease in it, which I didn't want to spill, so I navigated carefully, one step at a time. Suddenly, there was a gust of wind. The paper fluttered and flew into my face. It made me tip the pan, so the pig slid against my chest. I was covered with grease. There was quite a scene when I got home.

Dogs followed me around for months. My mother tried to clean the stain as best as she could, but the smell stayed. At night I'd cover myself with that overcoat and sniff the roast and see all those pigs on the sidewalk.

It is raining. It is Sunday. A gray afternoon in late fall. My radio is turned down low. I am on the bed reading. Time has stopped. I have a deep sense of well-being. I love the rain, which prevents me from going out to play.

I no longer remember the name of the book, or what year this was, but such moments spent with books are my happiest memories. I started reading early, because my father had a large library. There were serious books even in my room. They made me curious. First I turned the pages looking for pictures, then I looked at the words until with my parents' help I did learn how to read. By the time I was ten I was in love with books.

My friends read too. We liked Westerns, mysteries, adventure stories, comic books. Most of these books were published before the war and their supply was limited. It was possible, and this eventually happened to me, to have read all the books available in our circle. They could not be purchased in stores or taken out of libraries. We got the books from older people. Then we passed them around. There were long stretches of time, however, when there was nothing new to read. I had to turn to my father's library. I read Zola, Dickens, and Dostoevsky out of sheer boredom at first. Then I was hooked. *Oliver Twist* I liked very much. *Great Expectations* was even more wonderful. Thomas Mann's *Magic Mountain* was impossible to read. I loved the Serbian folk ballads and poems, but other poetry left me cold.

That need to read has never left me. I still read all kinds of books on all kinds of subjects. Consequently, I know only a little about a great many things. I could live and die in a good library, and I don't particularly respect great learning. I'm suspicious of the pedantry that kind of learning is prone to. Still, it seems impossible that one wouldn't want to know what's inside books.

Reading and imagining; imagining far away places and possible lives for oneself. So many places, so many lives! Who wouldn't want to relive again those hours of reverie when some great work of literature got hold of one's imagination?

Then there was music. My radio was always on. I discovered American jazz and couldn't get enough of it. Late at night, the radio would pick up the U.S. Army stations in Germany and Austria. This is the world I want to inhabit, it occurred to me. The world of Johnny Hodges and Lester Young playing the saxophone, and Billie Holiday singing.

During the day, my mother who was a voice teacher, an opera singing teacher, often had her conservatory students over to the house for lessons. I knew, by the age of five, most of the major operatic arias. I even sang them to myself as I played with my toys, which gave my mother the idea that I was destined to be a classical musician. The consequences were terrible. I had two years of violin lessons followed by two years of piano, and they were pure torture.

It wasn't just the instrument that gave me trouble, but the carrying case, too. I never saw another one like it. It was made of heavy wood, and it was big and heavy. The handle was on top instead of on the side, as was customary. It was made of brass, and there were other brass ornaments on the box. "It looks like a baby coffin," concluded one of my friends after examining it. He was right. Everybody who saw it thought the same thing. People shook their heads when I came down the street.

My teacher lived on the other side of town, so I had a long walk with that thing. To make me look even more ridiculous I wore an overcoat that reached down to my feet. It was somebody else's. I looked like a little old man. I remember my teacher's room, how quiet it was and cold. She would say nothing until the first few screechy notes of my violin, then her eyes would fill with horror, and she would start shouting.

This all ended when my brother jumped on the violin, which I had "carelessly" left on the bed. That was my version. The real story is much more perverse. I saw him jumping on the bed, bouncing himself off the way you would do off a trampoline. He did that all the time. One day I got the idea. I put the violin under one of the blankets. It splintered into hundreds of pieces when he landed on it. I had to pretend I was grief-stricken, terribly upset, and so on. Still, I don't think I completely fooled them. Violins were very expensive, and my mother realized by that time that my heart was not in it. So, there was no mention of getting me another one.

Still, I liked classical music well enough. She took me to a lot of concerts and opera performances. If her students were not around singing, she'd be practicing scales herself. When my father was around he sang, too. Operatic arias, Serbian folk songs, Hungarian gypsy songs, Russian ones—someone was always singing. My mother even sang folk songs on the radio. I thought she was terrible. Too refined to sing the hick songs right—the way my father knew how to do after a couple of bottles of wine. As it happens, he too had at one time studied singing at the conservatory. That's how they met. They even gave a couple of concerts together, sang Mozart duets.

"Your father was not serious," my mother told me over and over again as I was growing up. She said he spent all his time in taverns singing and raising hell. A good-hearted man, but totally unreliable, according to her. He'd step out to the corner to get a beer and be gone for two days. The first time it happened, she went out of her mind with worry and anger, but then she got used to it. He'd get so drunk and exhausted he would have to literally crawl home on all fours. In his expensive suit, his fine Italian felt hat, and English shoes—what a sight! All the neighbors would stick their heads out of their windows and enjoy themselves. "There goes George Simic crawling back to his wife," someone would say and they'd all laugh. I did, too, on hearing the story, which infuriated my mother. "You'll end up like your father," was her opinion.

Or even worse, I could end up like one my father's brothers. There were three, and as far as my mother was concerned only the youngest, Boris, who wanted to become an opera singer, was okay. The oldest one, Mosha, was criminal element pure and simple. The middle one, Mladen, was, despite his charm, also basically a crook. His two sisters were bitches. My grandfather was a nasty old man; my grandmother on the father's side an illiterate, superstitious peasant woman.

All this meant I hardly ever saw my father's family. Whenever I went there, I went alone with plenty of warning not to listen to what they say. My grandfather, for example, liked to make irreverent comments. He'd make fun of priests, politicians, Serbian national heroes—everything everybody held sacred. I loved listening to him. He made me laugh, and my grandmother fed me. Even he had a warning for me about Mosha. He threw him out of the house when he was still in grade school. This was hard to believe, but everybody assured me that it was true. Mosha was a bad man, but the stories my grandfather told me about him were very funny.

Mosha once had a job as a streetcar driver on the line that went past my grandfather's house. When he saw any member of the family waiting at the stop, he would drive right by shaking his fist. Luckily, he didn't last long on that job. One night after the streetcars stopped running, he took his girlfriend for a ride through the dark, sleeping streets of Belgrade. They went at top speed with him clanging the bell continuously. The whole city woke up. He was fired.

I met Mosha for the first time when I was twelve years old. He had just come out of prison. As the Russians and Yugoslav Communists were taking over Belgrade, he who had never had any political interests whatsoever had proclaimed himself a royalist in one of the taverns on the outskirts. Not a wise thing to do. In any case, there he was in our house inquiring about news of my father. A tall, handsome man in an elegant gray winter overcoat who addressed both me and my mother with great politeness. Not at all what I had been led to believe.

My mother's family was very different. They were what you call "respectable." They lived in apartments cluttered with fine old furniture, oil paintings, and thick Persian carpets. They never used bad language. When there was something the children were not supposed to understand they spoke French among themselves. They lived in fear, constant fear of everything. If I happened to sneeze, my grandmother on my mother's side would immediately put me to bed. "Oh my God! Oh my God!" she'd go around wringing her hands. She buried three of her six children, so she had plenty of reasons to expect the worst.

Still, it made the life around her constraining. She lived one floor below us, babysat for my mother, and often cooked for us. I loved her very much. She was kind and she could show affection much more than my mother ever could. At the same time, she was so unhappy. Her life had been miserable. She married a young officer who gambled away most of her money, gave her six children, and then retired at an age of forty to his native village. She struggled financially, and kept up appearances. My grandfather made occasional visits to Belgrade, but for all practical purposes they lived apart. There was resentment in the air and deep unhappiness.

In the meantime, I was in big trouble. Without anyone knowing, I had stopped going to school. The school that I attended and liked one day turned me away. Unknown to me, they had changed school districts, and the day I arrived to begin my sixth grade, they told me that I was now supposed to go to another school on the other side of town. When I presented myself there the next day, they had no record of me. I was advised to stay home a couple of days and return on Monday, by which time my file should be there and I could be placed in the proper class. Well, I never went back. At first I only wanted to prolong my summer vacation. I kept postponing the day of my return, so that weeks went by until it became impossible to go back. My mother knew nothing about this. I'd leave every morning for school and return with the rest of the children in the afternoon. It was the middle of January when somebody finally figured out that I was unaccounted for, and sent the cops after me.

While the weather was still balmy it was rather pleasant to roam the streets and parks of Belgrade, but then the rains came and the cold weather. If I was lucky and had managed to steal some money from my mother's purse, I went to the movies. Otherwise, I shivered in various doorways. The cold, clear days were better. I paced the city from one end to the other to keep warm and time passed quickly. At times, I'd be so preoccupied with my thoughts and worries, I'd walk past the outskirts and far into the countryside. I remember one such terrifying moment, turning around and seeing the city in the distance.

The movies also had their terrors. These were shabby, old

movie palaces with rat-eaten red velvet curtains and creaky wooden seats. They were cold and drafty in the morning. The customers were other truant children, university students, and tired-looking people who must've worked the night shift. They'd fall asleep immediately and then wake up in the middle of the film, their faces wild-eyed with incomprehension.

Often I, too, had no idea what was going on, although I paid attention. Some of these movies were ancient. It was hard to know whether the weather was always foul or the film was so old, grainy, and badly lit that it only looked that way. The people on the screen spoke French or English, and the subtitles were either faded or they didn't make much sense. After a while, I'd simply give up and just watch. There would always be some beautiful young woman I would fall in love with a little and try to commit her every gesture to memory. Otherwise, nothing much happened in these films. People sat around talking interminably. How one longed to see them on a train, or even better on an ocean liner. At times there were glimpses of strange cities. Streets full of people rushing off somewhere. Some were black and some were even Chinese. I saw schools as they had been a hundred years ago. Places where orphans were sent and where they beat you with a stick. I saw these movies again and again until I could say the English words, without understanding them, and could visualize each scene down to the minutest detail. I spent hours going over these scenes in my mind, inserting myself in the life of its heroes and sharing in their adventures.

My own situation was desperate. I couldn't even talk about it with my closest friends. For some reason they were still in the old school. They had no idea what I was doing. I had to pretend and invent elaborate lies about my activities in school. In fact, I lied all the time. It was a relief when they caught me and officially expelled me for truancy.

Still, all in all, what an adventure! I knew every corner, every storewindow in that city. I can still see clearly each dusty item in a poor shoe-repairer's window on a street in a quiet, residential neighborhood. I would stop by every time I was in the area and examine that window with the leisure of someone who has nothing else to do.

Once, looking into that window, I saw my mother reflected in the glass hurrying by on the other side of the street. I held my breath and continued to study the wooden shoes and the cans of shoe polish, which somehow I knew were empty. They had a foreign brand name. "Kiwi" I said to myself. I said it again many times.

"You're going to America some day to live with your father," people told me. I never believed it for a moment. It didn't seem possible that I could ever leave this street, this dusty store window where my mother had just passed. I was afraid to turn around. It was fine staying there just as I was.

In retrospect, it's lucky I did go to America. Had I stayed, I would have ended up in a reform school. Some of my friends did. I was certainly no better. When I went back to school the following September, one grade behind my old classmates, I hated the place. I knew it was just a matter of time before I'd get in trouble again.

In the summer I was usually packed off to my grandfather in the country. This was my mother's father, who had a house and a big orchard in the village where he was born. He lived there alone most of the time taking care of himself as best as he could. By the time I knew him, my grandfather had been in retirement almost thirty years. He was a distinguished-looking, vain and humorless man. His father was a bishop. He himself was an officer who took part in the assassination of a Serbian king in 1905.

With other young officers he broke into the royal bedroom and found the king and the queen hiding in the closet or under the bed—I forget which. The king asked for mercy, offered gold, promotions. My grandfather didn't actually shoot them, or so it was said in the family, but who the hell knows! The next day he was promoted to captain by the new king.

He had a short and distinguished military career. He was made colonel in the First World War after he took his troop into an attack one snowy night. He said he was cold in his tent, couldn't sleep, and wanted to warm himself by leading a charge.

After the war ended, the king pensioned him off in his fortieth year. Didn't want the hothead around. Kept an eye on him, too. Local yokels inducted to be police spies watched him nap under the huge oak tree in his back yard. He wore a straw hat, a white suit, and used a cane to keep away the village dogs.

It was torture staying with him. As he was a hypochondriac, there were all kinds of dietary prohibitions and obsessions with cleanliness. As for conversation, his only topics were his imaginary maladies and the clergy. He hated priests. Later on, when his wife died he wouldn't allow one at the funeral. It was because of his father, people said. A first class son of a bitch. The priests were as bad as generals, was his opinion. Scum of the earth.

There was a local priest famous in the area for riding everywhere on his black horse. He'd ride past our house often, slowing down each time to greet my grandfather. The old man under the oak tree made no acknowledgment of his presence. It embarrassed me. Everywhere I went in the village people gave me a funny look. The kids teased me about my crazy grandfather. I even got into a couple of fights about it. Even though I spent almost every summer in that place I never made any friends there. I felt superior coming from the city, and the kids my age felt superior because of their knowledge of country ways.

I couldn't wait for the summer to end. There were always important changes in the pecking order waiting for me in my neighborhood. One had to be reinstated into that world again. There were even new words, slang expressions one had never heard of before and which everybody used all the time. I'd be afraid to ask what they meant. I'd hear them every day, even use them myself, but it took weeks before I was in the know. In the meantime, I felt like a foreigner, as I was to feel so many times in my life.

What my secretive mother didn't tell me was that there was a good chance we would be leaving Yugoslavia. She had applied for a passport, since the relationship between Yugoslavia and United States had improved enough for the Communists to permit a few people to leave. The problem was that there was an American quota, a long waiting list for Yugoslavs applying to emigrate to the United States. One just had to wait, but my mother was afraid to wait in Belgrade because the authorities occasionally changed their minds and took the passports away. The moment she got ours, she decided to leave for Paris the very same night. Her brother was living there. We would stay with him or he would help us while my father, who was already in America, would send us money and support us while we waited for the visa.

I was playing basketball in the neighborhood that day in June 1953 when my mother summoned me and told me that we were going on vacation immediately. This was very strange. There had been nothing said earlier about a vacation on the coast. She was packing feverishly, wanted me to hurry up too, and make no noise. "Don't ask so many questions," she kept saying over and over.

"Why are we taking so many suitcases?" I wanted to know. Why were all the relatives coming to see us with tears in their eyes? Why was it that I was not permitted to say goodbye to my friends? I was confused. My mother's gone crazy, I thought. We had plenty of certified lunatics in the family to serve her as a model. My great aunt Marina, for example, or whatever she was to me! She wore old-fashioned dresses, sang and smiled to herself, and never went out. By the time I was ten, I knew there was something wrong with people like that.

Our train left at ten that night, but only the next day as we were approaching the Italian border did my mother reveal to me the true destination of our journey. I was stunned. Before I could get over it, we were in Trieste, that long-yearned-for, almost mythical Trieste. At the train station we bought some ice cream. All around us people spoke Italian. It seemed incredible. The Milan station was even bigger. I ate some sandwiches and drank my first Coca-Cola. Little by little, I was beginning to enjoy myself and look forward to what came next.

It took us almost two days to reach Paris. We were exhausted. My uncle met us at the station. We were taken to a small, seedy hotel where we took a tiny room with one large bed and one window. My mother and brother slept on the bed, and I slept on the floor. That's how we lived for one full year. It was a shock. We were poor, I realized. That first evening strolling along the Champs-Elysées, and many times afterwards, I became aware that our clothes were ugly. People stared at us. My pants were too short. My jacket was of an absurd cut. Waiters in cafés approached us cautiously. We had the appearance of people who do not leave a tip. In stores they eyed us as potential shoplifters. Everybody was surprised when we brought out the money. Even young girls at the open market selling apricots kept raising the bills to the light. After a couple of weeks in France, I knew I had a new identity. I was a suspicious foreigner from now on.

My mother wasn't going to buy us any new clothes. "You'll get everything new in America," she kept telling us. That took much longer than we expected. By the end of the summer, it was clear we might remain in Paris for a while. She thought the best thing for my brother and me was to attend school and learn French. I had studied the language in school in Yugoslavia and knew just enough to feel embarrassed every time I opened my mouth. For my brother it was easier. He was only eight years old and didn't care how it came out.

The school we were enrolled in was for children who were not meant to have a higher education. The French weed out the dummies at an early age and consign them to a permanent, inferior status. I felt pretty inferior myself. I couldn't do the schoolwork even on this level. The teachers were not helpful. It was as if they did not really believe that I could not speak French. Perhaps I was just pretending, trying to make a fool of them! They kept giving me zeros. In every subject, on every test and written assignment, I got a zero. At first I was upset and tried harder, but the zeros kept coming, so I gave up.

My classmates took no interest in me. The rare few who did were the troublemakers, the class idiots. I made friends with that bunch, which only confirmed my teachers opinion of me. I was now one of the hopeless. They told me so themselves many times in front of the class, while I counted the flies on the ceiling and debated in my mind the pros and cons of punching them in the mouth.

One of the advantages of being in school, as far as my mother was concerned, was that we got free lunch there. The rest of the time we cooked in my uncle's tiny apartment, or we ate sandwiches in our hotel room. We almost never ate in restaurants. We didn't have much money, and my mother was a type of person who didn't care what she ate. The only experience of French cuisine that I had was at school. I held a high opinion of our cooks that my classmates didn't share. They thought the food was fit for pigs, which meant that I got to eat their portions too. I especially loved the thick vegetable soup that everybody else hated. I'd have three or four plates of it. This made it difficult to stay awake after lunch. Once I fell asleep drawing a plaster statue of some Greek goddess. "Simic! Simic!" I still hear Monsieur Bertrand hollering.

That school year lasted a hundred years and it was always raining, it was always cold! You don't have to believe me, but that's how it was. Always gray, always drizzly!

To make things even worse I have an ear infection and am in terrible pain. My mother is taking me to a hospital on the other side of Paris because someone knows a doctor who will, supposedly, take good care of me. He is going to pierce my eardrum and let the pus out. That's what she tells me on the way. She's an expert because that's what they did to her when she was a little girl. She even describes the length of the needle they used. You might think my mother has a streak of cruelty in her, but that's not it. She is just dopey.

We are riding in a metro that is crowded with people going to work. Nobody looks very happy, but it's clear to me they're not suffering from earaches. They seem solid and have the arrogance of people who are at home. This is their city. The beautiful women have their powdered noses raised high. There's a smelly foreigner with a head full of pus on this train.

The hospital is old. It has a high wall and a guarded gate just like a military prison. You can tell a lot of people died in it. The walls inside are peeling, and the floors are dirty. The nurses are all in a foul mood. The patients in the crowded waiting room look resigned. Some of them have their eyes closed.

We sit and wait. I'm in great pain. I sit staring at the floor. Then I stare at somebody's shoes. Time has no meaning. This must be what eternity is all about. A pair of man's shoes worn by an old woman you contemplate forever and ever.

When we finally see the doctor, he's cheerful. A good-looking guy flirting with the nurses even as we come in. No needles for me today, just some penicillin and codeine. Yugoslavs are such wonderful people, he assures us. He knows, he's been there to some kind of conference. He also likes Marshall Tito. One of the world's great leaders. We agree completely. Yes, yes, an "homme magnifique."

All of a sudden, he's puzzled! How come we left beautiful Yugoslavia, and so forth? My mother tells him about my father in America, her longing to be reunited with her husband, but we can see he's thinking. Are we some kind of Nazi collaborators, or worse? Who else would leave Yugoslavia, which, as everybody knows, is heaven on earth?

This sort of thing happens often. The leftists think we must be Fascists, and the rightists that we are Commies. Explaining our family history makes it even worse, especially the part about my father leaving during the war for Italy when only Nazis could travel. Even I have to admit it sounds fishy. Our doctor is no longer friendly, and the nurses, too, eye us suspiciously.

On the street it's still raining. My ear is still hurting, but I'm happy there was no needle. And besides, I have an excuse not to go to school, for a few days at least.

Our only entertainment in Paris was walking. We walked even in the rain to get away from our tiny room. The moment our dinner was over—which was usually very early—we'd take off. If the weather was good, we'd ride the metro to some distant point and then walk back from there. Every day we'd chose another part of the city. The idea was eventually to see all of Paris, which we certainly did. Still, there were favorite areas like the one around the Opera, or the fancy shops on Rue

Saint Honoré. We each had a favorite shop window. We'd go see them every week the way other people went to the movies. They were mostly clothing stores and car showrooms. One of us would stand admiring the display, while the other two would grow impatient and start walking away after a while.

I also walked alone. Late in the evening as my mother and brother were falling asleep, I'd slip out of the room, supposedly to get some fresh air, and go roaming. At that hour I always went to the Champs-Elysées, which was a short distance away and usually busy late into the night. There were, of course, many movie houses and cafés, but there were also nightclubs, the Lido being the most famous one. I'd stand outside watching people going in and out. They could have been movie stars for all I knew. They wore dark glasses at night, which impressed me tremendously. I bought a cheap pair, which I wore while watching the beautiful women and their elegant beaus stumble tipsily toward their limousines. I hung around as if expecting them to invite me along. Nobody ever said a word to me, but that was all right. It was better than lying on that hard hotel floor listening to my mother and brother snore and talk in their sleep.

Once or twice I forgot myself. Suddenly it was very late. The night had turned cold, the great avenue was empty, and its cafés and movies all closed up. I'd hurry home taking the Avenue Victor Hugo, which was equally deserted and very dark as it was lined with big trees that obscured the street lights. I couldn't see a thing and I was cold. Then, I remembered to remove my glasses. It was a little better. A street of massive old buildings, every one of its windows dark. It was a beautiful moment. I had a very clear sense of myself existing—alone, deeply moved.

Some nights I went to the movies with some of the bad boys from school. My mother let me go, thinking it would improve my French. She had no idea of the company I was keeping. At first it was to the movies we went. Afterwards we only pretended to do that, and went instead to Pigalle and Place Blanche to look at the hookers. We began to dress up too. I wore a tie, kept my hair slicked down, and smoked cigarettes in the French manner, with the butt hanging from the corner of my mouth. Nobody took us seriously. We had no money for the girls. We were hoping for charity, love at first sight. The problem was that we had to be home by a certain hour. Whatever opportunities offered themselves after midnight, we were never to find out.

These French boys I hung around with were very nice. They came from poor families. Now that they were doing badly in school they knew their lives would be hard. They had absolutely no illusions about that. In the meantime, they had the street smarts, the humor, and appetite for adventure that reminded me of the friends I had left behind. Even with my limited French, we understood each other perfectly. They'd kid me about this or that, but it was all good-natured. Of course they knew everything about what goes on in Paris.

One afternoon I went to a nudie show with a friend. I remember that we thought about it for a long time before we actually got the courage to do it. We were afraid they would turn us away, laugh us off. This was one of the cheapest houses. Nobody asked any questions. We found ourselves in an almost empty theater. We sat right in front. There was a show with a couple of singers and a comedian. The women were ancient, or so it seemed to us. Huge thighs and busts and plenty of rolls of fat in between. From where we sat we could see the stretch-marks and scars on their bodies. They wore diamond-studded pasties and G-strings. The whole thing was shabby, badly done. I felt embarrassed. We didn't stay for the whole show.

The most important thing we did in Paris was study English. My mother found out that there were free night classes, twice a week, given by the World Church Service. All three of us went. Previously, I don't believe I knew ten words of English. My mother knew some, but not much. In any case, here we were in a class with a bunch of refugees from all over Eastern Europe and a very friendly American minister as a teacher. I worked hard. I liked the language immediately.

We began buying the *Saturday Evening Post* and *Look* magazine to practice reading. I understood little of what I read but the pictures and advertisements were very interesting. The American colors were so bright. One didn't see such yellows, reds, and oranges in Europe. The pictures of children terrified me. They looked so clean, so happy. The girls often had freckles. They smiled a lot. Everybody smiled. The old people, the movie stars, the politicians, all had their mouths stretched from ear to ear. In France nobody smiled like that. Certainly not the barbers. I remember a Norman Rockwell-like cover of a little redheaded kid in a barber's chair with a smiling barber bending over him with scissors. The barbers in Paris gave me dirty looks when I walked in to have one of my rare haircuts.

When we went to the American Embassy for the obligatory physical examination given to every immigrant, I expected the doctor to be smiling. He looked glum while listening to my chest. I must be very sick, I told myself. None of these Americans smiled. It was clear, I would be rejected. My brother and mother would go to America, and I'd stay in France dying from some incurable disease in a crowded and filthy state hospital.

Weeks passed before we got the results of the examination. In the meantime, we worried and turned the pages of American magazines, studying the cars, the baked hams, the rich desserts. The summer was approaching. We walked all the time. One evening, just after dusk, on the fashionable Avenue Victor Hugo, we saw Prince Paul, the brother of the dead Yugoslav King. My mother went up to him to say we were Yugoslavs. I remember an impeccably dressed, elderly man bowing stiffly to my mother and asking me my name. I could tell he didn't care one way or the other.

In those days, both in Paris and America, we ran into famous politicians, people who were responsible, if anyone was truly responsible, for Yugoslavia's troubles. Here would be a face you remembered from a newspaper, signing some treaty with Hitler or whatever, now sitting in somebody's kitchen slicing salami. It was hard to believe they were the same people. They looked ordinary and talked nonsense like everybody else. They expected to go back soon. Their villas and bank accounts would be restored. Great crowds would welcome them. "You were right! You were always right," the people would shout. They didn't like what my mother and I had to say about Yugoslavia. They insisted that nothing had changed since they left.

In June of 1954, or thereabouts, we received our American visas. It took a few more weeks to book our passage. The World Church Service paid for our trip and in style. We were to sail on the *Queen Mary* on August 5. What excitement! "You'll be starting a new life," everybody said, even our grocer.

Our remaining days in Paris dragged on. My mother took us to museums daily so we'd remember the great art treasures of France. We also started eating in modest neighborhood restaurants. At night we went to the movies, watching the American films for clues to our future.

In school I had flunked everything except drawing and music, so I avoided my friends. I was ashamed. After the terror of waiting for the results of my physical, I felt a bit more optimistic, but not completely. Who could be sure I was not going to be a failure in America?

III

The *Queen Mary* was all lit up the night we boarded. It was huge and a veritable labyrinth on the inside. We were traveling in the cheapest class but the accommodations seemed luxurious to us. It took a couple of days to discover that we were not supposed to leave our class. There was a door with a sign that spelled it out. I snuck through it once, walked through the magnificent Cabin Class, and made my way to the First Class. There were shops and restaurants there as elegant as anything they have in Paris. I saw ladies in evening gowns cut so low their breasts were about to fall out, men in dark suits smoking cigars, little children who wore neckties and looked snotty. I remember a bejeweled old woman in a wheelchair pushed by a very beautiful nurse in white. It didn't take long before a steward spotted me ogling and directed me politely back to the Tourist Class.

We had no complaints about our class. Far from it. Our

cabins were small and windowless but otherwise comfortable. The food was excellent and there was a new film shown every day. Everybody was friendly, and in a good mood, especially in the beginning of the trip.

A day or two after we left Le Havre there was a storm. It started during the night. The ship heaved and creaked as if about to come apart. It was impossible to sleep and many people got seasick. In the morning only a few showed up for breakfast. By the afternoon, with the storm still raging, the movie theater was empty. They showed the movie anyway. The boat rocked, the waves pounded its sides, but the people on the screen went on talking with perfect composure.

My mother was back in the cabin throwing up, but my brother and I refused to stay in bed. We liked the food so much, we didn't allow ourselves to get sick. We roamed our section of the ship. It was difficult to walk, of course. We had to hold on to the walls and railings. It never occurred to us to be scared. We sat in the empty lounge for hours watching the waves crest and slide under the ship. There was a lot of water out there. It was absolutely amazing. We couldn't get over it.

The next day the storm subsided. The sky was cloudless. The chart outside the purser's office indicated the progress of our voyage. We were more than halfway across. The next day we were even closer. We kept asking the crew when we would be able to see the land.

The sighting occurred at night. By the time we rose in the morning the land was clearly visible. We were speeding into the New York harbor. After breakfast, everyone was on deck. We began to make out details on the land. There was a road on which a car was traveling. Everybody kept pointing to it! Next, there were some neat white houses. One even had laundry hung out to dry in its back yard. Then a fishing boat came by. There were a couple of black men on deck, waving. Pretty soon there were small boats everywhere. We could see the Statue of Liberty. I think a cheer went up.

What stunned me, left me speechless with excitement, was the first sight of Manhattan with its skyscrapers. It was just like in the movies, except this was the real thing. The enormous city before us with its docks, its big ships, its traffic on the outer highways, its billboards and crowds. My father was out there somewhere waiting for us. We tried to spot him. We didn't realize we would have to go back down and spend hours clearing immigration. With our past experiences of border crossing, we were a bit nervous. You never knew. What if they pulled a surprise on us and sent us back to Yugoslavia?

My father waited past the customs. A tall man. We recognized him from the pictures. We waved. He waved back. He was wearing a white suit under which we could see a blue shirt and suspenders. Very American we thought. He smoked a long thin cigar and smiled in a friendly way.

Then, the confusion of embraces and kisses, the emotion of his seeing my brother for the first time, the search for a porter, the wait for a taxi, and everybody talking at the same time. It was all incredible and wonderful! The trash on the streets, the way people were dressed, the tall buildings, the dirt, the heat, the yellow cabs, the billboards and signs. It was nothing like Europe. It was terrifically ugly and beautiful at the same time! I liked America immediately.

In the hotel room another surprise awaited us. There was a television set. While my mother and father talked, my brother and I sat on the floor and watched a Dodgers-Giants game. I remember who was playing because my brother fell in love with baseball that afternoon and with the Dodgers in particular, and insisted on being outfitted immediately with a baseball cap and glove.

That evening, after a stroll around Times Square and Broadway, we went to a restaurant where we dined on hamburgers, french fries, and milk shakes, followed by banana splits. I don't know what my mother thought of the meal, but we loved it. American food is kid's food and no kid in the world can resist it. "Remember this day," my father kept saying. Indeed, it was August 10, 1954. Tomorrow he was going to buy us American clothes and shoes and all sorts of other things.

Who could possibly sleep? My mother and brother did. My father and I watched TV and talked. It was still early. "Let's go for a walk," he said. The hotel was only a couple of blocks away from Times Square. We found ourselves there again, watching the crowd. I felt comfortable with my father right away. He never treated anyone younger differently. He talked to everybody the same way. He'd talk to the five-year-old selling lemonade on the street as if he were the head of a major corporation.

We ended up in a jazz club that night. It was called the Metropole, on Broadway around Forty-eighth Street. A long narrow room with a bar on one side and small booths on the other. The bandstand was just above the bar. There were six black musicians blasting away.

We took a booth and my father ordered some whiskey for himself and ginger ale for me. This must have been some day for him too. I was all absorbed in the music. This was definitely better than my radio. It was heaven.

We stayed a long time. My father even gave me a few sips of his whiskey. Between sets we talked. I told him about my life, and he told me about his. This was just the beginning. We spent many nights together like that. My father loved the night life. He was happiest in bars and restaurants. In the company of friends and with something good to eat and drink, he'd glow. It was pure joy to be around him then. He was full of life and interesting talk. I didn't want to go to bed, but we finally had to.

"This is wonderful," he said. He always wanted to come to America and had a chance to do so when in 1926 he won some kind of scholarship to Columbia University, but then he didn't, to his everlasting regret and for reasons that were entirely trivial. "Even in prison in Italy," he told me, "I sat in solitary confinement dreaming of New York."

One morning the Germans took him out into the courtyard at daybreak, and he figured they were going to shoot him. There was a squad of armed soldiers and an officer with them, but then a photographer with a tripod came and took several pictures of my father standing against the wall. He had no idea what for.

"I want to see New York before I die," he told the Germans as they were leading him back to his cell.

My father was still employed by the same telephone company he worked for in Yugoslavia. Their headquarters were in Chicago, but, he spent all his time on the road. Whenever one of their client companies needed more telephone lines, my father was sent to examine the facilities, draw up the blueprints, and stay there till the job was completed. As it was, he spent the years 1950–54 moving from one small town to another, spending in each place anywhere from a couple of months to a year. He had no home. At the time we arrived, he was working in Middletown, New York. After his vacation was over, and having found an apartment for us in Queens, he went back to Middletown. I went with him.

The idea was, I would study English on my own and not enroll in school till the second semester. We would spend the week in Middletown and come to New York on weekends. That's what we did. I stayed in the rooming house while my father worked. In the evenings we ate out, then either went to the movies or came back to our room to talk and drink wine.

My father, as was his custom, had a lot of books, two trunks full. At that time his ambition was to write a critical history of Marxism, so most of the books were on that subject. He read late into the night and took voluminous notes. He made occasional comments about the project as he told me about his life. There was his life, and there was Marxism and Fascism and everything else. He was trying to make sense of it all.

His stories were tremendously entertaining. He was also interested in my own. We had a lot of catching up to do. What made it exciting for me is that for the first time in my life I could be absolutely frank. I told him everything, and he did the same to me. We were both, in our own way, very lonely people. The ten years that we didn't see each other made it difficult to reestablish our relationship on a father-son basis. It was much easier to be friends, to talk like friends. When people overheard us they were shocked. "The way that boy speaks to his father!"

During this time he was teaching me English. The first book I read in English was Whittaker Chamber's *Witness*. I don't remember a thing about it today, but at the time it gave me the confidence necessary to attempt to read others. When in New York, my father would spend Saturday mornings going from bookstore to bookstore. He bought books, and it was understood I could pick some for myself. I did that often, picking out something much too difficult for me. I read Hemingway and Twain and God-knows-what-else! It was a slow process, since I had to look up a lot of words in the dictionary, and there were long passages that I simply didn't understand. Still, I had so much time to myself while he was at work.

My return to school terrified me. It had been a long time since I was properly a student. I had no confidence in my ability. I also had no idea what grade I would be in. I would see young people my age going to school and I would shudder. The way I spoke English anybody could tell immediately I was a foreigner.

The closer Christmas came and the beginning of the second semester, the more miserable I became. My father was still a lot of fun, but the mood at home was tense. It was clear my parents were not getting along. The ten years of separation, plus their completely different personalities, made them strangers. Whatever one liked, the other did not. My mother, for example, had no interest in things American. She had already found some Yugoslavs, was seeing them, and aside from wanting to improve her English so that she could get a job, she had no curiosity about this country. Since my brother and I sided with my father, there were constant conflicts. She grew jealous. "You don't love me anymore," she'd blurt out. "We have more fun with him," we'd make the mistake of saying.

Still, for a while appearances were preserved. We sat around the dinner table making plans for the future. My brother and I would go to college and that sort of thing. I had my doubts, but I said nothing.

The high school I was supposed to attend was in Elmhurst, Queens. My parents had gone there to make inquiries. I was invited to come shortly before the classes resumed after the New Year and take some tests so I could be placed in the proper grade.

I didn't sleep the night before the appointment. My father was back in Middletown. It was a windy and bitterly cold morning, and the walk from our place to the school was very long. I was numb with cold and terror when I arrived.

As usually happens in life, things turned out quite differently from what I had anticipated. First of all, there was no question of writing for a transcript to Belgrade or Paris. The European education system is very different, and it would be very difficult to interpret such a document whenever it eventually arrived. So they made it simple. They gave me an IQ test, and as for the rest, they just asked me to write down the subjects I had studied in Europe.

That was easy enough. I wrote down things like algebra, physics, French, Russian, world history, biology. They asked me a couple of questions in each area and in the process found out that in Paris we had read Homer and Virgil. That did it. I was made a second semester junior on the spot. The whole process did not take more than a couple of hours.

I was greatly relieved. I still had some apprehension about actually doing the schoolwork, but this was a miraculous beginning. My love for America was infinite. No more Monsieur Bertrand and his crummy jokes at my expense. Even the Yugoslav teachers had given me hard times after I stayed back. School was not for dummies like me, they reminded me daily. Years later, I heard they were incredulous when told that I had gone on to college. "That little bum! Don't Americans have any sense?"

The school itself was amazing. Newtown High School may have been the model for the movie *Blackboard Jungle*. I had met all kinds of juvenile delinquents in my life, but never so many. This was like reform school. The teachers had their hands full maintaining discipline. If you kept your mouth shut, as I did, you passed all your subjects.

I remember a large class in something called "Hygiene." I sat in the last row playing chess with a black kid. Up front the teacher was arguing about something with a couple of punks in leather jackets. That's the way it was every day, half of the class harassing the teacher while the other half daydreamed. I never did any work. Nobody called on me. I don't think I even had a clue what I was supposed to do, but I kept my mouth shut. I received a B for my silence at the end of the semester.

The other classes were more or less the same. In English, the old lady who was our teacher kept trying to read aloud one of Edgar Allan Poe's tales. The class, against her objections, provided the sound effects. There were sinister creaking doors and coffin lids, clocks ticking at midnight, and the wind blowing through the ruined tower. She pleaded with us to stop. When we were reading *Julius Caesar,* it was the same. More sound effects and muffled laughter.

I came to see her once after class to ask for an extension on my term paper, blaming the delay on my ignorance of the English language. "Don't worry," the poor woman told me. "I know you're a good boy." I certainly was. I behaved in class and did my homework. The girls interested me, but I was too shy to speak to them in my heavily accented English. As for the boys, many of them were trouble-bound and I'd had enough of that for a while. Also, I had no time to hang around. I was working after school and all day Saturdays.

It was a terrific job as far as I was concerned. I worked for a small company that supplied special screws for airplanes. I helped the stock clerk. I counted screws. These screws were very expensive, so you had to be super-careful counting them. I was. It wasn't difficult and I got paid. I bought a cheap phonograph and my first jazz records. On Sundays I went to Manhattan and the movies. I was beginning to feel very comfortable in America.

The big event that spring was buying a television set. It was a huge twenty-one inch model that my father and I had a hell of a time lugging from the store. Once we turned it on, it stayed on. We watched television all the time. It was good for our English, everybody said. It certainly was. I stopped reading books and just watched TV. Everything interesting from breakfast shows to late, late movies. I think that it was while watching television that my brother and I started speaking English to each other. We heard certain expressions on TV and wanted to use them immediately.

I am surprised how quickly we felt at home in the United States. My father's attitude had a lot to do with it. He thought America was the most exciting place on earth and wanted us to share his excitement. He had no desire to go back to Yugoslavia. He wanted us to be real Americans. My mother, on the other hand, had always retained the conviction that Europeans were superior. She missed Europe. I did not. I was a flop there. Here I had managed to finish a grade. I had a job and summer was coming.

Then we had another surprise. My father's request for a transfer to the company's headquarters, which he didn't expect to be approved, suddenly came through. We were moving to Chicago. From now on we would live together, see him all the time, and have a normal life.

I wasn't entirely happy about being uprooted again, nor was my mother. She worried about leaving New York, where there were more opportunities to find work in the music business. She was trying to resume her career as a voice teacher but had no luck. Still, she also desired some kind of regular family life. There really was not much choice. It was decided that my father and I would go first, find an apartment, and then my mother and brother would follow.

It was late in June of 1955 when we traveled to Chicago on the train called *The Twentieth Century*. We were going in style, sleeping in Pullman berths and taking our meals in the fancy dining car. In Chicago we took a room at the elegant Hotel Drake on Michigan Avenue. The lake was right outside our window. There was a beach we could go to and many fine restaurants and nightclubs in the area. We spent the first two weeks enjoying life and not making the slightest effort to look for a place. When my mother called, we told her it was difficult, the city was so big, and so on.

Again my father and I talked and talked. I was beginning to have a much clearer picture of our family background from these late-hour conversations.

My great-grandfather Philip, for example, was a blacksmith in a small village in Serbia. My great-grandmother had died in childbirth and he himself took care of his son and daughter. It seems he didn't have any relatives in the area. Earlier, his own father, or his grandfather, had migrated to Serbia from Montenegro. My father didn't know for sure.

I liked the stories about this great-grandfather of mine,

one of them especially! How he had not been paying taxes for some time, and how one day the cops came in force to arrest him. He pleaded with them not to take him away and make his children orphans. He even had a suggestion. What if they were to give him a part-time job at the police station, make him a deputy or something, so he could earn some extra money and pay his taxes?

Well, the cops being local fellows and knowing Philip, took pity on him. At the police station the arrangements were made. He was issued a rifle and was even given a small advance on his pay for other purchases related to his new duties. There were tears of gratitude on his part, everyone was moved, and after many handshakes Philip left. He made his way straight to the tavern where he stayed for three days raising hell. When he was thoroughly out of his mind, he made the waiters at gunpoint carry four tables outside. Then he ordered that the tables should be stacked, one on top of the other, with a chair and a bottle of booze at the very top. There he climbed, drunk as he was. A crowd had gathered by then. There were gypsies, too, fiddling and banging on their tambourines. When he started shooting his rifle and shouting that no Simic was ever going to be a stupid cop, the police showed up. They beat the daylights out of him and threw him in jail.

Philip's son, my grandfather Zika, went to Vienna and Prague while still a very young man to learn the tool-and-die trade. Upon his return just before the First World War, and over the years, he became the best craftsman in that trade in Belgrade. Following the war, his skills were in such demand that he even became wealthy for a while. Temperamentally, though, he was just like his father. He couldn't keep money. He hated all middle-class values and institutions. Politicians, priests, and schoolteachers were on his list of contemptible beings. He had absolutely nothing in common with my other grandfather, but here they were in agreement. "I only love waiters," I heard him say once.

Nevertheless, he married a schoolteacher's sister. Radojka, my father's mother, bore Zika four children and died from consumption when my father was twelve. As he was the oldest, he took care of the younger ones. Even in the last days of his life, while he lay dying in the hospital in Dover, New Hampshire, my father often spoke of his mother. She sang beautifully and played "every instrument," as he put it. He still remembered the songs she taught him and would try to sing them with tears in his eyes:

> Three meadows and no shade anywhere to be found,
> Three meadows, just an old bare pear tree . . .

I forget the words exactly, but he never did. He never got over her death. His sorrow for her and her short, unhappy life was greater for him seventy years later than the thought of his own imminent extinction, which he took with a kind of detached amusement.

The relationship to his father was more complex. He told me many times that he didn't want to be the bastard his father had been to him. But then, he'd tell me some story about the two of them going drinking together and listening to the gypsies, and there'd be a lot of affection for his father. All Zika's children—and there were two more from another marriage—had that love-hate relationship with their father.

Be that as it may, here in Chicago my father and I were continuing to live it up. Every night we told ourselves that tomorrow we'd start looking for a place, but we never did—not, in any case, till my mother informed us that she was coming in a week to help us look. In the meantime, my father was running out of money. He was supposed to resume working soon, but the first paycheck would not be coming for a while and his savings were gone. One morning he visited a loan company, where he finagled a huge loan. We still had a few days left before my mother's arrival and we spent them partying. The way my father tipped waiters and bought books and clothes for us made it look as if we would soon be broke again. He'd give a waiter ten dollars the moment he came to our table with the menus, and ask him to take the damn things away and bring us instead a good bottle of wine, and not to bother us until we called him.

That recklessness of his both attracted and drove me crazy. Years later in New York, we once spent our monthly rent on a meal in a French restaurant. It was an expensive and fashion-able place. We were ushered without much ceremony to a tiny table in the back where we polished off our appetizers, main course, and a couple of bottles of wine rather quickly and un-consciously, absorbed as we were in some sort of intellectual argument. When the snotty waiter presented us with the bill, we both realized at the very same moment that 1) the service had been lousy; 2) we'd talked too much and hadn't really savored what we were eating and drinking; 3) we were in no rush to go anywhere. Without exchanging a word, we knew what the next step would be. My father informed the waiter that in place of a dessert we'd like to have the whole meal repeated, starting with the appetizers and the white wine. "The whole thing once again," I told him, too, just to make sure he understood. The waiter went away and came back, flustered, to ask us to repeat, please, what we'd said. So we did, and then resumed our talk. In time they brought the food, which we ate with an even greater appetite. By then the place was emptying. The waiters stood across the room watching us apprehensively. The boss and the cook finally came over with a bottle of fine cognac. "Do you always dine like this?" they wanted to know. "Only when we are hungry," my father assured them.

Three days after my mother arrived in Chicago we found an apartment in Oak Park, a suburb west of the city. My mother got in touch with some Serbians she knew, and they told her that Oak Park was a nice place to live. We took the el one morning, bought the local papers, and by the afternoon had our place. It was on the top floor of a three-story tenementlike building and had two bedrooms, a living room, and a fairly large kitchen. The neighborhood, with its tree-lined streets and one-family homes, was a good one, but the apartment was crummy. In their impatience to find a place, my parents didn't realize that there were railroad tracks just outside our back windows. All the trains leaving Union Station for points west roared by, rattling our pots and pans, and just about every-thing else. We were so close to the trains we could see the people in the dining car being served by black waiters. We could almost make out what they had on their plates. It didn't occur to my parents to move. I guess they were sick and tired of moving. We stayed and made the best of the situation.

I was enrolled in Oak Park's high school. That's the one Ernest Hemingway attended. The teachers reminded us of that every day. My mother found a job in Marshall Field's department store as a seamstress. My brother was in third grade. He was doing great, playing baseball and speaking English better than I did. Life could have been normal, except that my parents were snapping at each other or didn't speak to each other for days. I had the unenviable task of passing messages between them. As far as I was concerned, they were both right and both wrong. I loved them equally, but I hated having them under the same roof.

My new school was no joke. One had to study, do homework every night, and be prepared to answer intelligently in class. My classmates were mostly children of professional people and had the confidence and ability of well brought up young people. They were very nice to me. I think I was the only foreigner in school and so I was a curiosity. Soon enough I began leading the life of a typical small-town teenager. I went to football games, and hung around the drug stores and hamburger joints frequented by my classmates.

I had some interesting teachers too. My English teacher, a man by the name of Dolmetsh, took time with me. He realized I was a voracious reader, so he supplied me with books. He gave me Joyce's *Portrait of the Artist as a Young Man* and a number of other contemporary classics to read. A French teacher gave me contemporary French poets. In addition to the books I got in school, I discovered the public library. I couldn't believe that one had the right to take all those wonderful books and records home. I went almost every day and got a new load.

I was also beginning to be interested in painting. I drew, did water colors, and even some oil paintings that year. This was an important activity. I discovered modern art and its aesthetic. I never had any illusion that I had much talent, and I stopped painting when I was twenty-six years old, but some of the things I did show a fairly good knowledge of the abstract expressionist idiom, and some taste.

In school, of course, I gravitated toward students who were interested in the arts. One day, two of my friends confessed that they wrote poetry. I asked them to show it to me. I wasn't impressed with what I saw. I went home and wrote some poems myself in order to demonstrate to them how it's supposed to be done. At first, the act of writing and the initial impression were exhilarating. Then, to my astonishment, I realized that my poems were as stupid as theirs were. I couldn't figure it out. It made me pay attention to poetry in a different way. I went through a couple of anthologies trying to divine the secret. I tried writing again, but it was still no good. To be sure, it all began with my wanting to impress my friends, but then, in the process of writing, I discovered a part of myself, an imagination and a need to articulate certain things, that I could not afterwards forget.

I graduated from high school in August of 1956 instead of June. I was missing some credits and had to take classes in summer school. I was supposed to go to college, but there was no money. My father spent everything he earned and had accumulated large debts. Neither he nor my mother were very good at planning for the future. They never thought of finding out what college cost and what options there were. It didn't take me long to realize that I was on my own.

At the end of the summer I found a job as an office boy at the *Chicago Sun Times* and started attending night classes at the University of Chicago. I took the el to the city early in the morning and returned late at night. It was a lonely time. All my school friends were in college. And my parents were fighting all the time. The atmosphere was oppressive. I spent as little time as possible at home.

At the *Sun Times* I met a young writer, a fellow a little older than I, who had a furnished room on the North Side. That gave me an idea. I got a room too. It was in a basement of a tenement next to the hot-water boiler. I went home early that night and told my parents I was moving out. They were stunned. For once, they ganged up on me. I was too young, too inexperienced, and so on.

I couldn't be budged. I ended up yelling at them that I

hated their fighting, couldn't bear the sound of their voices any more. The next morning I was gone. Shortly after, my parents came to visit me, individually. They were appalled by the squalor I was living in. I didn't notice it. I was happy.

At work I was promoted to a proofreader, a union job. I made an excellent salary. I bought books, jazz records, and I painted. When I was broke, I went home or my father took me out to eat. Our relationship was fine once again. We did what we did best. We stayed out late drinking and talking.

I also made friends in the neighborhood and got to know some girls at the university. The people I met all had ambitions in the arts, and that encouraged my own efforts. I painted more than I wrote, but poetry was my secret ambition. I was getting obsessed with it. I wanted to know everything about it instantly. I read all the time. A friend introduced me to the poems of Lowell and Jarrell. Another gave me the works of Stevens and Pound. At night, when I was not attending classes, I went to the Newberry Library to read the French Surrealists and literary magazines.

Even today I'm amazed by the change I underwent in that four to five year period. One moment, so it seemed, I was an unremarkable Yugoslav schoolboy, and the next moment I was in Chicago writing poetry in English, as if it were the most normal thing to do.

My first poems were published in the winter 1959 issue of the *Chicago Review*. They were written about a year and a half earlier. The two published poems differ a great deal. They don't seem to be written by the same poet. That was typical of my work at that time. I liked so many different kinds of poetry. One month I was a disciple of Hart Crane, the next month only Walt Whitman existed for me. When I fell in love with Pound I wrote an eighty-page long poem on the Spanish Inquisition. It was awful, but the effort I put into it was tremendous. I'd work all night on it, go to work half-asleep, and then drag myself to night classes. I probably produced more poetry in the years 1956–61 than in all the years since. Except for a few poems, it was all bad, and one day I had the pleasure of destroying them all.

I was in the Army, had been in the service for six months, when in the winter of 1962 I asked my father to send me the folder with the poems. I sat down on my cot the evening they arrived and read them. Everybody else in the barracks was shining shoes, playing cards, listening to their radios, and I was reading my collected poems. Perhaps being away from them for so long and being in such different circumstances then made me see them clearly. I noted all the obvious influences and awkward writing. There were at least a couple of hundred pages. I ripped them up in a hurry and threw them in the garbage. They embarrassed me. I still wanted to write poetry, but not that kind.

Now I look more affectionately on that Chicago period. Had I gone to college like everyone else, had I stayed at home with my parents, perhaps it wouldn't have turned out quite the way it did. Being alone like that, I had to justify my existence in my own eyes. It was obvious I wasn't going to succeed in life in the usual way, so I wrote and painted.

Otherwise, I had no idea what was to become of me. My previous life had taught me that making plans is a waste of time. My father used to ask me jokingly, "Where are we going to immigrate next?" Anything was possible in this century. The experiment was still in progress. People like him and me were its laboratory animals. Strangest of all, one of the rats was writing poetry.

The year is 1943 or 1944, and this one of my earliest memories. I think it was winter. My mother has taken me to the opera, to a performance of Mozart's *Marriage of Figaro.* It's the first act, and Susanna and Figaro are in an eighteenth-century salon, singing. On several tables there are candelabras with lit candles. At one point, Susanna brushes against one of the candles and the scarf she's wearing over her shoulders catches fire. The audience gasps. She stops singing and stands still with that scarf on fire. Figaro, without missing a beat, quickly snatches the scarf, throws it on the floor, and stamps on it like a Spanish dancer. All along he's singing that beautiful music . . .

Reading Philosophy at Night

*It is night again around me; I feel as though there had been
lightning—for a brief span of time I was entirely in my element
and in my light.*

　　　　　　　　　　　　　　　　　　—*Nietzsche*

*The mind loves the unknown. It loves images whose meaning is
unknown, since the meaning of the mind itself is unknown.*

　　　　　　　　　　　　　　　　　　—*Magritte*

I wore Buster Keaton's expression of exaggerated calm. I
could have been sitting on the edge of a cliff with my back to
the abyss trying to look normal.

Now I read philosophy in the morning. When I was younger
and lived in the city it was always at night. "That's how you
ruined your eyes," my mother keeps saying. I sat and read late
into the night. The quieter it got, the more clearheaded I
became—or so it seemed to me. In a sparsely furnished room
above an Italian grocery, I would be struggling with some
intricate philosophical argument that promised a magnificent
insight at its conclusion. I could sense it with my whole being.
I couldn't put the book away, and it was getting really late. I
had to be at work in the morning. Even had I tried to sleep,
my head would have been full of Kant or Hegel. So, I
wouldn't sleep. At some point I'd make that decision. I'd be
sitting there with the open book, my face reflected dimly in
the dark windowpane, the great city all around me grown

Written for the special issue of *Antaeus* on the pleasures of reading
and first published in 1987.

quiet. I was watching myself watch myself. A very strange experience.

The first time it happened I was twenty. It was six o'clock in the morning. It was winter. It was dark and very cold. I was in Chicago riding the el to work seated between two heavily bundled-up old women. The train was overheated, but each time the door opened at one of the elevated platforms, a blast of cold air would send shivers through us. The lights, too, kept flickering. As the train changed tracks, the lights would go out for a moment and I would stop reading the history of philosophy I had borrowed from the library the previous day. "Why is there something rather than nothing?" the book asked, quoting Parmenides. It was as if my eyes were opened. I could not stop looking at my fellow passengers. How incredible, I thought, all of us being here, existing.

Philosophy is like a homecoming. I have a recurring dream about the street where I was born. It is always night. I'm walking past vaguely familiar buildings trying to find our house, but somehow it is not there. I retrace my steps on that short block of only a few buildings, all of which are there except the one I want. The effort leaves me exhausted and saddened.

In another version of this same dream, I catch a glimpse of our house. There it is, at last, but for some reason I'm unable to get any closer to it. No lights are on. I look for our window, but it is even darker there on the third floor. The entire building seems abandoned. "It can't be," I tell myself in horror.

Once in one of these dreams, many years ago, I saw someone at our window, hunched over as if watching the street intently. That's how my grandmother would wait late into the night for us to come home, except that this was a stranger. Even without being able to make out his face, I was sure of that.

Most of the time, however, there's no one in sight during the dream. The facades of buildings still retain their pock-marks and other signs of the war. The streetlights are out and there's no moon in the sky, so it's not clear to me how I am able to see all this in complete darkness. The street I am walking on is long, empty, and seemingly without end.

Whoever reads philosophy reads himself as much as he reads the philosopher. I am in dialogue with certain decisive events in my life as much as I am with the ideas on the page. Meaning is the matter of my existence. My effort to understand is a perpetual circling around a few obsessive images.

Like everyone else, I have my hunches. All my experiences make a kind of untaught ontology, which precedes all my readings. What I am trying to conceptualize with the help of the philosopher is that which I have already intuited.

That's one way of looking at it.

> The Meditation of yesterday filled my mind with so many doubts that it is no longer in my power to forget them. And yet, I do not see in what manner I can resolve them; and, just as if I had all of a sudden fallen into very deep water, I am so disconcerted that I can neither make certain of setting my feet on the bottom, nor can I swim and so support myself on the surface. I shall nevertheless make an effort and follow anew the same path as that on which I yesterday entered, i.e., I shall proceed by setting aside all that in which the least doubt could be supposed to exist, just as if I had discovered that it was absolutely false; and I shall ever follow in this road until I have met with something which is certain, or at least, if I can do nothing else, until I have learned for certain that there's nothing in the world that is certain. Archimedes, in order that he might draw the terrestrial globe out of its place, and transport it elsewhere, demanded only that one point should be fixed and immovable; in the same way I shall have the right to conceive high hopes if I am happy enough to discover one thing only which is certain and indubitable.

I love this passage of Descartes; his beginning again, his not wanting to be fooled. It describes the ambition of philosophy in all its nobility and desperation. I prefer this doubting Descartes to the later one, famous in his certainties. The poetry of indeterminacy still casts its spell. Of course, he's greedy for the absolute, but so is everybody else. Or are they?

There's an Eastern European folk song that tells of a girl who kept tossing an apple higher and higher until she tossed it as high as the clouds. To her surprise the apple didn't come down. One of the clouds got it. She waited with arms outstretched, but the apple stayed up there. All she could do was plead with the cloud to return her apple, but that's another story. I like the first part when the impossible still reigns.

I remember lying in a ditch and staring at some pebbles while German bombers were flying over our heads. That was long ago. I don't remember the face of my mother nor the faces of the people who were there with us, but I still see those perfectly ordinary pebbles.

"It is not 'how' things are in the world that is mystical, but that it exists," says Wittgenstein. I felt precisely that. Time had stopped. I was watching myself watching the pebbles and trembling with fear. Then time moved on and the experience was over.

The pebbles stayed in their otherness, stayed forever in my memory. Can language do justice to such moments of heightened consciousness? Speech is always less. When it comes to conveying what it means to be truly conscious, one approximates, one fails miserably.

Wittgenstein puts it this way: "What finds its reflection in language, language cannot represent. What expresses 'itself' in language, we cannot express by means of language." This has been my experience many times. Words are impoverishments, splendid poverties.

I knew someone who once tried to persuade me otherwise. He considered himself a logical positivist. These are people who remind you, for example, that you can speak of a pencil's dimension, location, appearance, and state of motion or rest but not of its intelligence and love of music. The moment I hear that, the poet in me rebels and I want to write a poem about an intelligent pencil in love with music. In other words, what these people regard as nonsense, I suspect to be full of imaginative possibilities.

There's a wonderful story told about Wittgenstein and his Cambridge colleague, the Italian economist Piero Sraffa. Apparently they often discussed philosophy. "One day," as Justus Hartnack has it, "when Wittgenstein was defending his view that a proposition has the same logical form as the fact it depicts, Sraffa made a gesture used by Neapolitans to express contempt and asked Wittgenstein what the logical form of that was? According to Wittgenstein's own recollection, it was this question which made him realize that his belief that a fact could have a logical form was untenable."

As for my "logical" friend, we argued all night. "What cannot be said, cannot be thought," he claimed. And then—after I blurted out something about silence being the language of consciousness—"You're silent because you have nothing to say!" In any case, it got to the point where we were calling each other "you dumb shit." We were drinking large quantities of red wine, misunderstanding each other totally, and only stopped bickering when his disheveled wife came to the bedroom door and told us to shut up.

Then I told him a story.

One day in Yugoslavia, just after the war, we made a class trip to the town War Museum. At the entrance we found a battered German tank, which delighted us. Inside the museum one could look at a few rifles, hand grenades, and uniforms, but not much else. Most of the space was taken up by photographs. These we were urged to examine. One saw people who had been hanged and people about to be hanged. The executioners stood around smoking. There were piles of corpses everywhere. Some were naked. Men and women with their genitals showing. That made some kid laugh.

Then we saw a man having his throat cut. The killer sat on the man's chest with a knife in his hand. He seemed pleased to be photographed. The victim's eyes I don't remember. A few men stood around gawking. There were clouds in the sky.

There were always clouds, blades of grass, tree stumps, bushes, and rocks no one was paying any attention to. In one photograph the earth was covered with snow. A miserable, teeth-chattering January morning and someone making someone else's life even more miserable. Or the rain would be falling. A small, hard rain that would wash the blood off the hands immediately, that would make one of the killers catch a bad cold. I imagined him sitting that same night with feet in a bucket of hot water and sipping tea.

That occurred to me later. Now that we had seen all there was to see, we were made to sit on the lawn outside the museum and eat our lunch. It was poor fare. Most of us had plum jam spread on slices of bread. A few had lard sprinkled with paprika. One kid had nothing but bread and scallions. I guess that's all they had at his home that day. Everybody thought it was funny. Someone snatched his thick slice of black bread and threw it up in the air. It got caught in a tree. The poor kid tried to get it down by throwing stones at it. He kept missing. Then he tried climbing the tree. He kept sliding back. Even our teacher who came to see what the commotion was all about thought it was hilarious.

As for the grass, there was plenty of it, each blade distinct and carefully sharpened, as it were. There were also clouds in the sky and many large flies of the kind one encounters in slaughterhouses, which kept pestering us and interrupting our laughter.

And here's what went through my head just last night as I lay awake thinking of my friend's argument:

The story you told him had nothing to do with what you were talking about.

The story had everything to do with what we were talking about.

I can think of a hundred objections after all these years.

Only idiots want something neat, something categorical—and I never talk unless I know!

Aha! You're mixing poetry and philosophy. Wittgenstein wouldn't give you the time of day!

"Everything looks very busy to me," says Jasper Johns, and that's my problem, too.

I remember a strange cat, exceedingly emaciated, that scratched on my door the day I was scratching my head over Hegel's Phenomenology of the Spirit.

Who said, "Whatever can be thought must be fictitious"?

You got me there! How about a bagel Hegel?

Still and all . . . And above all! Let's not forget "above all."

Here's what Nietzsche said to the ceiling: "The rank of the philosopher is determined by the rank of his laughter." But he couldn't really laugh. No matter how hard Friedrich tried, he couldn't really laugh.

I know because I'm a connoisseur of paradox. All the good-looking oxymorons are in love with me and come to visit me in my bed at night.

Have a tomato Plato!

Wallace Stevens has several beautiful poems about solitary readers. "The House Was Quiet and the World Was Calm" is one. It speaks of a "truth in a calm world." It happens! The world and the mind growing so calm that truth becomes visible.

It must be late at night "where shines the light that lets be the things that are"—the light of insomnia. The solitude of the reader of philosophy and the solitude of the philosopher drawing together. The impression that one is thinking and anticipating another man's subtlest turns of thought and beginning to truly understand.

Understanding depends on the relationship of what we are to what we have been: the being of the moment. Consciousness stirring up our conscience, our history. Consciousness as the light of clarity and history as the dark night of the soul.

The pleasures of philosophy are the pleasures of reduction—the epiphanies of hinting in a few words at complex matters. Both poetry and philosophy, for instance, are concerned with Being. What is a lyric poem, one might say, but the recreation of the experience of Being. In both cases, that need to get it down to its essentials, to say the unsayable and let the truth of Being shine through.

History, on the other hand, is antireductive. Nothing tidy about it. Chaos! Bedlam! Hopeless tangle! My own history and the history of this century like a child and his blind mother on the street. She mumbles, talks to herself, sings and wails as she leads the way across some busy intersection.

You'd think the sole meaning of history is to stand truth happily upon its head!

Poor poetry. Like imperturbable Buster Keaton alone with

the woman he loves on an ocean liner set adrift on the stormy sea. Or an even better example: Again drifting over an endless ocean, he comes across a billboard, actually a target for battleship practice. Keaton climbs it, takes out his fishing rod and bait, and fishes peacefully. That's what great poetry is. A superb serenity in the face of chaos. Wise enough to play the fool.

And always the contradictions: I have Don Quixote and his windmills in my head and Sancho Panza and his mule kicking in my heart.

That's just some figure of speech. Who could live without them? Do they tell the truth? Do they conceal it? I really don't know. That's why I keep going back to philosophy. I want to learn how to think clearly about these matters.

It is morning. It is night. The book is open. The text is difficult, the text is momentarily opaque. My mind is wandering. My mind is struggling to grasp the always elusive, the always hinting—whatever it is.

It, it, I keep calling it. An infinity of "it" without a single antecedent—like a cosmic static in my ear.

Just then, about to give up, I find the following on a page of Heidegger: "No thinker has ever entered into another thinker's solitude. Yet it is only from its solitude that all thinking, in a hidden mode, speaks to the thinking that comes after or that went before."

For a moment it all comes together: poetry, philosophy, history. I see—in the sense of being able to picture and feel— the human weight of another's solitude. So many of them seated with a book. Day breaking. Thought becoming image. Image becoming thought.

Notes on Poetry and Philosophy

It is the hardship of the times that before an artist can fashion an icon he must compose the theology that his icon will reinforce.
—*Harold Rosenberg*

Some sort of Academy of Fine Arts from which they stole the bust of the philosopher Socrates so he may accompany them on what was to be a night of serious drinking.

It was heavy. The two of them had to lug it together. They went from tavern to tavern like that. They'd make Socrates sit in his own chair. When the waiter came, they'd ask for three glasses. Socrates sat over his drink looking wise.

Later, in a low dive where gypsies were playing, a couple of drunken women joined them. They loved their "friend." They kept kissing Socrates and trying to make him drink wine. His mouth turned red. He could have been bleeding.

They left Socrates, as the day was breaking, at a streetcar stop. The number 2 would arrive full of sleepy factory workers, the doors would open, and there'd be the Greek philosopher with his blind gaze and his bloodied mouth, waiting on the sidewalk to be taken up.

KNIGHTS OF SORROWFUL COUNTENANCE
SITTING LATE OVER DOG-EARED BOOKS

That was my father's story. Philosophy intrigued him all his life. He loved it. He made fun of it. He was the one who gave

---

Written as a commentary on an essay linking my own poetry with Heidegger's philosophy for *New Literary History* in 1989.

me Heidegger's *Being and Time*. We read its most difficult passages together and discussed the book endlessly.

"Amateur philosophers, the worst kind!" he used to say about us.

I continued to read Heidegger as his various works became available in English. The attraction was strong for a Surrealist—which is what I considered myself in those days. "Avant-garde is revolt and metaphysics," says Rosenberg. You cannot have great poetry without at least an attempt at one. That's how I understood the legacy of Rimbaud and Stevens. Heidegger made my own intuitions about the philosophical ambitions of modern poetry clearer to me.

The other appeal of Heidegger was his attack on subjectivism, his idea that it is not the poet who speaks through the poem but the work itself. This has always been my experience. The poet is at the mercy of his metaphors. Everything is at the mercy of the poet's metaphors—even Language, who is their Lord and master.

"O PARADISO!" MY POP SANG IN THE SHOWER

The twentieth-century poet is "a metaphysician in the dark," according to Wallace Stevens.

That sounds to me like a version of that old joke about chasing a black cat in a dark room. The room today is more crowded than ever. In addition to Poetry, Theology is also there, and so are various representatives of Western and Eastern Philosophies. There's a lot of bumping of heads in the dark. The famous kitty, however, isn't there. . . . Still, the poets continue to cry from time to time: "We got her folks!"

Unless, of course, it's the Devil himself they've got by the tail instead!

THE FISH IS SPHINX TO THE CAT

There is a major misunderstanding in literary criticism as to how ideas get into poems. The poets, supposedly, proceed in one of these two ways: they either state their ideas directly or they find equivalents for them. What is usually called philosophical poetry seems to be either a poetry of heightened eloquence or some variety of symbolism. In each case, the assumption is that the poet knows beforehand what he or she wishes to say and the writing of the poem is the search for the most effective means of gussying up these ideas.

If this were correct, poetry would simply repeat what has been thought and said before. There would be no poetic thinking in the way Heidegger conceives of it. There would be no hope that poetry could have any relation to truth.

IN A HEAD THIS OLD THERE'S A BLIND HEN THAT OCCASIONALLY FINDS A KERNEL OF CORN AND HER NAME IS LOVE

My poems (in the beginning) are like a table on which one places interesting things one has found on one's walks: a pebble, a rusty nail, a strangely shaped root, the corner of a torn photograph, etc. . . . where after months of looking at them and thinking about them daily, certain surprising relationships, which hint at meanings, begin to appear.

These *objets trouvés* of poetry are, of course, bits of language. The poem is the place where one hears what the language is really saying, where the full meaning of words begins to emerge.

That's not quite right! It's not so much what the words mean that is crucial, but rather, what they show and reveal. The literal leads to the figurative, and inside every poetic figure of value there's a theater where a play is in progress. The play is about gods and demons and the world in its baffling presence and variety.

In its essence an interesting poem is an epistomological and metaphysical problem for the poet.

THE WAY A CHILD STUDIES THE MINUTE HAND OF HIS WATCH

Back in 1965 I sent some of my object poems ("Fork" among them) to a literary magazine. They came back with a letter that said something like this: "Dear Mr. Simic . . . you're obviously a sensible young man, so why do you waste your time by writing about knives, spoons, and forks?"

I guess the editor's premise was that there were things worthy of poetry and that the fork in my hand was not one of them. In other words, "serious" subjects and "serious" ideas make "serious" poems, etc. He was just trying to give me fatherly advice.

I was surprised by the resistance some people had to these poems. "Back to things themselves," said Husserl, and the Imagist had the same idea. An object is the irreducible itself, a convenient place to begin, it seemed to me.

What appealed to me, too, was the discipline, the attention required, and the dialectics that went with it. You look and you don't see. It's so familiar that it is invisible, etc. I mean, anybody can tell when you're faking it. Everybody is an expert when it comes to forks.

Plus, all genuine poetry in my view is antipoetry.

LIKE A BARBER COLLEGE HAIRCUT

Poets think they're pitchers when they're really catchers.
—Jack Spicer

Everything would be very simple if we could will our metaphors. We cannot.

This is true of poems, too. We may start believing that we are recreating an experience, that we are making an attempt at mimesis, but then the language takes over. Suddenly the words have a mind of their own.

It's like saying, "I wanted to go to church but the poem took me to the dog races."

When it first happened I was horrified. It took me years to admit that the poem is smarter than I am. Now I go where it wants to go.

A SHORT ORDER COOK PEELING
METAPHYSICAL ONIONS

Heidegger says that we will never understand properly what poetry is until we understand what thinking is. Then he says, most interestingly, that the nature of thinking is something other than thinking, something other than willing.

It's this "other" that poetry sets traps for.

ETERNITY, THE PRESENT MOMENT, PLAYING WITH EACH OTHER

My hunch has always been that our deepest experiences are wordless. There may be images, but there are no words to describe the gap between seeing and saying, for example. The labor of poetry is finding ways through language to point to what cannot be put into words.

Robert Duncan had this to say about the pronoun "it," which for him was the most interesting word in the language, as it is for me:

> The gnostics and magicians claim to know or would know *Its* real nature, which they believe to be miswritten or cryptically written in the text of the actual world. But Williams is right in his "no ideas but in things"; for *It* has only the actual universe to realize *Itself*. We ourselves in our actuality, as the poem in its actuality, its thingness, are facts, factors, in which *It* makes *Itself* real.

Duncan is speaking out of the Romantic and occult tradition, but here he's close to Heidegger, who speaks of the "It" that gives Being, the "It" that gives Time.

The poem that thinks is a place where we open to "It." The poem's difficulty is that it presents an experience language cannot get at. Being cannot be represented or uttered—as poor realists foolishly believe—but only hinted at. Writing is always a rough translation from wordlessness into words.

VERY QUIET. PSSST.

> *We cannot say what reality is, only what it seems like to us.*
> —*Gaston Bachelard*

Every new metaphor is a new thought, a fragment of a new myth of reality.

Metaphor is a part of the not-knowing aspect of art, and yet I'm firmly convinced that it is the supreme way of searching for truth. How can this be? I don't know. I have never been able to figure it out to my satisfaction.

Poetry attracts me because it makes trouble for thinkers.

TO UNDERSTAND, IS THAT AGAINST NATURE, AGAINST GOD?

I like a poem that understates, that leaves out, breaks off, remains open-ended. A poem as a piece of the unutterable whole. To "complete," to pretend that it is possible to do so, (and here, too, I'm following Heidegger), is to set arbitrary boundaries to what is boundless.

Emily Dickinson's poems do that for me. Her ambiguities are philosophical. She lives with uncertainties, even delights in them. To the great questions she remains "unshielded," as Heidegger would say. The nature of presence itself is her subject. The awe of . . . the supreme mystery of consciousness watching itself.

Ideally then, a poem that speculates is full of mirrors . . . it measures the gap between words and what they presume to name . . . the gap between being and being-said.

LIKE THOSE BEAUTIFUL WOMEN ASLEEP A HUNDRED YEARS?

> *Something must be for something to be said.*
> *—Paul Ricoeur*

The world was going up in flames and I was making screeching noises on my violin. The baby Nero. Once walking to the market I saw people in a ditch with their throats cut. Then I got lice wearing a German helmet.

This used to be a famous story in my family. I remember those cold, hungry winters just after the war, with everybody huddled around the coal stove, talking and worrying late into the night. Sooner or later, inevitably, someone would bring up my German helmet full of lice as comic relief. Old people would have tears of laughter in their eyes. A kid dumb enough to walk around with a German helmet full of lice. They were crawling all over it! A blind man could see them!

I sat there saying nothing, pretending to be equally amused, nodding my head in agreement while thinking to myself, what a bunch of idiots! They, of course, had no idea how I got the helmet, and I wasn't about to tell them.

It was the day after the liberation of Belgrade. I was up in the fairgrounds by St. Mark's church with a few older boys, more or less snooping around. Then, all of a sudden, we saw them! Two German soldiers, obviously dead, stretched out on the ground. We drew closer to take a better look. They had no weapons. Their boots were gone, but there was a helmet, which had fallen off to the side. I don't remember what the others did, but I went for the helmet. I tiptoed so as not to wake the dead men. I also kept my eyes averted. I never saw their faces, even if sometimes I think I did. Everything else about that moment is still intensely clear to me.

GIUSEPPE VERDI, THE FAMOUS CHINESE-AMERICAN VENTRILOQUIST . . .

Poetry is not just "a verbal universe that looks inwardly on itself," as someone said. Neither is poetry merely a recreation of experience. "It was and it was not," is how the old storytellers used to begin their tales. It lies to tell the truth.

Mallarmé thought there were two kinds of language: *parole brute,* which names things, and *parole essentielle,* which distances us from things. One serves representation and the other the allusive, fictive world of poetry. He's wrong. It's not that clear-cut. If anything, it's both. Poetry is impure. I don't think Heidegger understands this either.

The poem is an attempt at self-recovery, self-recognition, self-remembering, the marvel of being again. That this happens at times, happens in poems in many different and contradictory ways, is as great a mystery as the mystery of being itself and cause for serious thought.

Chinese Boxes and Puppet Theaters

Consciousness is the only home of which we know.
—Dickinson

Two images come to mind when I think of Emily Dickinson's poems: Chinese boxes and puppet theaters. The image of boxes inside boxes has to do with cosmology, and theaters and puppets with psychology. They're, of course, intimately related.

The intimate immensity of consciousness is Dickinson's constant preoccupation. I imagine her sitting in her room for hours on end, with eyes closed, looking inward. To be conscious is already to be divided, to be multiple. There are so many me's within me. The whole world comes into our inner room. Visions and mysteries and secret thoughts. "How strange it all is," Dickinson must have told herself.

Every universe is enclosed in some other universe. She opens boxes, Pandora's boxes. There's terror in one; awe and ecstasy in the next one. She cannot leave the boxes alone. Her imagination and love of truth conspire against her. There are so many boxes. Every so often, she may believe that she has reached the last one, but on closer examination it proves to contain still another box. The appearances deceive. That's the lesson. A trick is being played on her as it is being played on all of us who wish to reach the truth of things.

"As above, so below," Hermes Trismegistus claimed. Emerson thought the same. He believed that clarity and heightened understanding would follow the knowledge of that primary

---

Written for an Emily Dickinson issue of the magazine *Ironwood* in 1986.

law of our being. Dickinson's experience of the self is very different. The self for her is the place of paradoxes, oxymorons, and endless ambiguities. She welcomed every one of them the way Emerson welcomed his clarities. "Impossibility, like wine, exhilarates," she told us.

Did she believe in God? Yes and no. God is the cunning of all these boxes fitting inside each other, perhaps? More likely, God is just another box. Neither the tiniest one nor the biggest imaginable. There are boxes even God knows nothing of.

In each box there's a theater. All the shadows the self casts and the World and the infinite Universe. A play is in progress, perhaps always the same play. Only the scenery and costumes differ from box to box. The puppets enact the Great Questions—or rather Dickinson allowed them to enact themselves. She sat spellbound and watched.

Some theaters have a Christian setting. There is God and his Son. There is Immortality and the snake in Paradise. Heaven is like a circus in one of her poems. When the tent is gone, "miles of Stare" is what remains behind. In the meantime, the Passion and Martyrdom of Emily Dickinson go on being played under the tent and under the open skies. There's no question, as far as I am concerned, that real suffering took place among these puppets.

In some other theaters the scenery could have been painted by De Chirico. In them we have a play of abstract nouns capitalized and personified against a metaphysical landscape of straight lines and vanishing points. Ciphers and Algebras stroll along "Miles and Miles of Nought" and converse. "The Truth is Bald and Cold," she says. Truth is a terrifying mannequin, as Sylvia Plath also suspected. This is the theater of metaphysical terror.

Death is in all the plays and so is this woman. Death is a kind of master of ceremonies, opening boxes while concealing others in his pockets. The self is divided. Dickinson is both on stage and in the audience watching himself. "The Battle fought between Soul and No Man" is what we are all watching.

That she made all this happen within the length of a lyric poem is astonishing. In Dickinson we have a short poem that builds and dismantles cosmologies. She understood that a poem and our consciousness are both a theater. Or rather, many theaters.

"Who, besides myself, knows what Ariadne is," wrote Nietzsche. Emily Dickinson knew much better than he did.

Visionaries and Anti-Visionaries

The work of art is a secret sign exchanged
between meaning and meaninglessness
—Octavio Paz

Here is that famous passage in Emerson's essay "Nature" on which all American visionary poetry is based:

> Crossing a bare common, in snow puddles, at twilight, under a clouded sky, without having in my thoughts any occurrence of special good fortune, I have enjoyed a perfect exhilaration. I am glad to the brink of fear . . .

He then goes on to say:

> Standing on the bare ground,—my head bathed into infinite space,—all mean egotism vanishes. I become a transparent eyeball; I am nothing; I see all; the currents of the Universal Being circulate through me; I am part or parcel of God.

The history of American poetry of the last hundred years can be seen as a dispute between poets who endorse Emerson's vision and poets who have no use for it. Walt Whitman and William Carlos Williams, for example, part company on that very issue.

There's a third group, too, made up mostly of New England poets who accept Emerson's experience but not his interpretation. They are suspicious that he might be giving an optimistic twist to his experience in order to protect himself against its meaninglessness and existential terror.

Delivered as a lecture to the Poetry Society of America in 1988 and published in the *Denver Quarterly* in 1989.

I call them visionary skeptics. Poets like Dickinson, Frost, and Stevens who have a lover's quarrel with Emerson and his Transcendentalism. I say a "lover's quarrel," because American literature is unimaginable without Emerson, and great poetry is equally unimaginable without some kind of metaphysics. All truly philosophical poetry is visionary. It speculates on the nature of ultimate reality, or rather, it wishes to embody it, to be the thing itself.

Let's look more closely at what Emerson says. A vision comes to him when he least expects it. He does nothing to prepare for it. Suddenly, a number of things happen. He feels an exhilaration. He is both happy and afraid. He's on the verge of a great insight. He sees himself with uncommon clarity. He is standing on the bare ground, while his head is about to float off. The moment he realizes his double nature his love of self vanishes. He sees that his "I" is nothing. For a moment he partakes in the ultimate reality, which for him is the knowledge that he is part of the cause of all existence.

Emerson is writing an instruction manual for visionaries. In a passage from the same text, which I omitted earlier, he says:

> In the woods, too, a man casts off his years, as the snake his slough, and at what period soever of life is always a child. In the woods is perpetual youth. Within these plantations of God, a decorum and sanctity reign, a perennial festival is dressed, and the guest sees not how he should tire of them in a thousand years. In the woods we return to reason and faith. There I feel that nothing can befall me in life,—no disgrace, no calamity (leaving me my eyes), which nature cannot repair.

There are not many poets in our tradition who did not convert to this view. Emily Dickinson did not. Nor did Frost or Stevens. For them Nature is opaque, inert, mute, and often malevolent. Nature transmits no message. It is a realm of endless ambiguity. For Dickinson the world in a moment of vision takes on the properties of oddness and unfamiliarity. At such times, we are made strangers to ourselves: "Nature is a haunted house," she says.

This is how it comes out in a poem:

There's a certain Slant of light,
Winter Afternoons—
That oppresses, like the Heft
Of Cathedral Tunes—

Heavenly Hurt, it gives us—
We can find no scar,
But internal difference,
Where the meanings, are—

None may teach it—Any—
'Tis the Seal Despair—
An imperial affliction
Sent us of the Air—

When it comes, the Landscape listens—
Shadows—hold their breath—
When it goes, 'tis like the Distance
On the look of Death—

There is such a moment at the end of a short winter day when the night already begins to shadow the last rays of light. How quiet must be the room in which such a vision takes place! The light growing old, wavering and yellowing as it makes its slow departure. The sense of witnessing a mystery, a sacred mystery, and the accompanying hurt, the ache of one's mortality.

Or perhaps nothing so well-defined! It's more like those moments when somebody asks what is bothering us, and we reply—nothing! What is this "nothing"? It is an awareness of a something that cannot be put into words. For Emily Dickinson it is not an insight that one has in moments of vision, but the loss of words, the awe, as she says, before that "Nothing which makes possible the presence of Everything."

For Emerson God is manifest in the visible. Nature is a finite extension of the infinite God. He says "Each particle is a microcosm, and faithfully renders the likeness of the whole." The point here is that God can be known, can be grasped, as it were. For Dickinson, on the other hand, God is infinitude, an incomprehensible immensity that overwhelms the individual human being. "A distant, stately lover," she calls him.

Here's a strange visionary poem of hers:

> Because I could not stop for Death—
> He kindly stopped for me—
> The Carriage held but just Ourselves—
> And Immortality.
>
> We slowly drove—He knew no haste
> And I had put away
> My labor and my leisure too,
> For His Civility—
>
> We passed the School, where Children strove
> At Recess—in the Ring—
> We passed the Fields of Gazing Grain—
> We passed the Setting Sun—
>
> Or rather—He passed Us—
> The Dews drew quivering and chill—
> For only Gossamer, my Gown—
> My Tippet—only Tulle—
>
> We paused before a House that seemed
> A Swelling of the Ground—
> The Roof was scarcely visible—
> The Cornice—in the Ground—
>
> Since then—'tis Centuries—and yet
> Feels shorter than the Day
> I first surmised the Horses' Heads
> Were toward Eternity—

"Death sets a thing significant the eye had hurried by," she says in another poem. Death here is a courtly lover who stops for her. Death stops, and time stops. She has an experience of the timeless moment very much like Emerson's, except that her description and her interpretation of it are very different. She stops in time and paradoxically takes a journey in the timeless moment. There she has the vision of the beginning and the end, and the experience is chilling.

"A suspicion like a Finger Touches my Forehead now and

then that I'm looking oppositely for the site of the Kingdom of Heaven," she writes. Indeed, she has the vision of an infinite universe of which God is only a small part. That's what Death proceeds to show her. For her there's only awe, infinite awe, big enough to swallow God.

With Robert Frost, too, we are a good distance from Emerson's Romantic idealism. Pronouncements like "Nature never wears a mean appearance," or "Nature stretches out her arms to embrace man, only let his thoughts be of equal greatness" must have amused Frost. Much of his poetry is a not-so-subtle polemic with Emerson and the Transcendentalists. He, the impoverished New Hampshire farmer, knows another truth. It is not the culture of Concord and Amherst that he gives us, but another, harsher New England. Not the "quaint natives" of Henry James, surely, but overworked farm people struggling with elementary problems of a bleak existence.

An Old Man's Winter Night

All out-of-doors looked darkly in at him
Through the thin frost, almost in separate stars,
That gathers on the pane in empty rooms.
What kept his eyes from giving back the gaze
Was the lamp tilted near them in his hand.
What kept him from remembering what it was
That brought him to that creaking room was age.
He stood with barrels round him—at a loss.
And having scared the cellar under him
In clomping here, he scared it once again
In clomping off;—and scared the outer night,
Which has its sounds, familiar, like the roar
Of trees and crack of branches, common things,
But nothing so like beating on a box.
A light he was to no one but himself
Where now he sat, concerned with he knew what,
A quiet light, and then not even that.
He consigned to the moon, such as she was,
So late-arising, to the broken moon
As better than the sun in any case
For such a charge, his snow upon the roof,

His icicles along the wall to keep:
And slept. The log that shifted with a jolt
Once in the stove, disturbed him and he shifted,
And eased his heavy breathing, but still slept.
One aged man—one man—can't keep a house,
A farm, a countryside, or if he can,
It's thus he does it of a winter night.

In other words, in a vast, mysterious, perhaps even meaningless universe, you keep yourself together by ritual. If solitude is the final reality, then all we have to make it bearable are these half-magical routines. Perhaps Emerson's metaphysics, too, is just a branch of magic? Perhaps all religion, all science, all philosophy in their essence are based on the principles of sympathetic magic? Frost is not averse to such perverse views. Here is what he has to say further:

The Most of It

He thought he kept the universe alone;
For all the voice in answer he could wake
Was but the mocking echo of his own
From some tree-hidden cliff across the lake.
Some morning from the boulder-broken beach
He would cry out on life, that what it wants
Is not its own love back in copy speech,
But counter-love, original response.
And nothing ever came of what he cried
Unless it was the embodiment that crashed
In the cliff's talus on the other side,
And then in the far distant water splashed,
But after a time allowed for it to swim,
Instead of proving human when it neared
And someone else additional to him,
As a great buck it powerfully appeared,
Pushing the crumpled water up ahead,
And landed pouring like a waterfall,
And stumbled through the rocks with horny tread,
And forced the underbrush—and that was all.

It's a funny poem, of course. The "it" that stands for the great other, finally, in answer to a prayer, manifests itself as a great buck that lunges past the speaker without seeing him, or acknowledging him. I like that "horny tread," that devil's tread! If this is the embodiment of Nature, it is not very reassuring! Nature is oblivious of us, the poem seems to be saying. We might just as well not be here at all as far as "it" is concerned.

> *Between names and reality there lies an abyss.*
> —*Octavio Paz*

There's no poet in this century who has had a clearer understanding of Emersonian tradition and its temptations and difficulties than Wallace Stevens. Or more precisely, what he understands are the mechanics of Emersonian vision. The visionary experience is the place where the questions of reality, imagination, knowledge, and belief all come together. In its essence the visionary experience is an epistomological problem. How do we know what we know, and how can we be sure that we are not deluding ourselves? Psychology and metaphysics are Stevens's constant preoccupations. The twentieth-century poet is a "metaphysician in the dark," he says. Many of his poems dramatize the full philosophical and existential implications of that predicament.

No Possum, No Sop, No Tatters

He is not here, the old sun,
As absent as if we were asleep.

The field is frozen. The leaves are dry.
Bad is final in this light.

In this bleak air the broken stalks
Have arms without hands. They have trunks

Without legs or, for that, without heads.
They have heads in which a captive cry

Is merely the moving of a tongue.
Snow sparkles like eyesight falling to earth,

Like seeing fallen brightly away.
The leaves hop, scraping on the ground.

It is deep January. The sky is hard.
The stalks are firmly rooted in ice.

It is in this solitude, a syllable
Out of these gawky flitterings,

Intones its single emptiness,
The savagest hollow of winter-sound.

It is here, in this bad, that we reach
The last purity of the knowledge of good.

The crow looks rusty as he rises up.
Bright is the malice in his eye . . .

One joins him there for company,
But at a distance, in another tree.

This is a kind of "bare commons" landscape. I wouldn't go
so far as to suggest that this is a critique of Emerson's vision,
because I firmly believe that Stevens, usually, in poems of this
kind, begins with a particular experience. I mean to say that
these details don't sound made up. Still, it is impossible for
anyone who stands before a barren New England landscape
not to think of Emerson sooner or later. As is so often the case,
Stevens is curious about the ways in which we interpret our
experience, the ways in which we make it meaningful, and at
what cost.

We are in the dead of winter. The landscape is barren. The
sky is hard. The wind is savage. The dry vegetation is like a
crowd of the infirm outside some holy shrine. The crippled,
the blind, the deaf and dumb coming to beg. When it gets this
bad, Stevens says, we console ourselves by claiming that
thanks to it we now know its opposite (the good) in all its
purity. It doesn't fool the crow, however. He can see through
our game; thus the "malice in his eye." Abashed, we join the
hard realist but "at a distance, in another tree." We cannot live
where the crow lives. Where the crow lives there's no such
thing as bad or good.

A more ambitious example of this dialogue with Emerson
is a late poem, "The Course of a Particular." In terms of what
I have been talking about, it is both anti-visionary and vision-

ary in that it rejects the now familiar Transcendentalist rhetoric, and yet, when all that is discarded, the poem attempts to convey its own version of the truth.

The Course of a Particular

Today the leaves cry, hanging on branches swept by wind,
Yet the nothingness of winter becomes a little less.
It is still full of icy shades and shapen snow.

The leaves cry . . . One holds off and merely hears the cry.
It is a busy cry, concerning someone else.
And though one says that one is part of everything,

There's a conflict, there is a resistance involved;
And being a part is an exertion that declines:
One feels the life of that which gives life as it is.

The leaves cry. It is not a cry of divine attention,
Nor the smoke-drift of puffed-out heroes nor human cry.
It is the cry of leaves that do not transcend themselves,

In the absence of fantasia, without meaning more
Than they are in the final finding of the ear, in the thing
Itself, until, at last, the cry concerns no one at all.

Again it is winter and the wind is blowing. The hardness of the wintry landscape is made bearable by the almost-human cry of the leaves. The leaves cry, as they must in a philosophy in which one is part of everything. But, as one listens, straining not to project one's own emotions into the sound the leaves make, one begins to sense a separation. One is not part of everything. To continue to believe so is "an exertion," an effort of the will. Instead, one feels something else beginning to emerge, a something that gives Being to all these things. No, the sound of the leaves doesn't signify divine attention, heroic ideal, or human cry. Rather, freed of these imaginings, one intuits "the thing itself," the Kantian "ding an sich," which Emerson, too, claimed to have known. The difference is that for Stevens the absolute reality beyond the mind signifies nothing. One cannot say it is "indifferent," since that would just personify it further. We simply are not its concern. We are not "part and parcel" of Nature as Emerson claims.

What I want to note in conclusion is the central place that these distinctions have for American poetry with philosophical ambitions. I am surprised that this has not been more understood. Now that Emerson has been rediscovered by certain critics, everybody has been made an Emersonian, even a convinced materialist like William Carlos Williams.

In a late poem of his, "The Clouds," Williams wrestles with the issue of Transcendentalism, considers its attractions, rejects it as an obfuscation, an escape from here and now, and then concludes, surprisingly, by saying, how, nevertheless, its temptation remains.

It's not that we are forever stuck with Emerson, it's just that we cannot have great poetry without some vision of truth. The three poets I have looked at briefly share in common their suspicion of Emerson, but it is that suspicion that impels them to construct their own metaphysics. Truth is not stable, truth needs to be rediscovered continually, their example proves. The American poet is the high trapeze artist in a visionary circus where the lights have been turned off.

Caballero Solo

the adulterers who love each other truly
on beds as lofty and long as ocean liners

I first read Pablo Neruda's poems in Dudley Fitts's huge *Anthology of Contemporary Latin-American Poetry*. This must have been in the fall of 1958. I remember a long day of loneliness and rain in New York City, a day of aimless walking around, culminating in the discovery of that book in the used bookstore on Fourth Avenue. I was astonished at what I had in my hands. I didn't know such a book existed.

One of the first poems I happened to read in it, later that evening in a corner saloon where I had stopped for beer, was Neruda's "Walking Around" in H. R. Hays's beautiful translation:

> It so happens I am tired of being a man.
> It so happens, going into tailorshops and movies,
> I am withered, impervious, like a swan of felt
> navigating a water of beginnings and ashes.
>
> The smell of barbershops makes me weep aloud.
> All I want is a rest from stones or wool,
> all I want is to see no establishments or gardens,
> no merchandise or goggles or elevators.
>
> It so happens I am tired of my feet and my nails
> and my hair and my shadow.
> It so happens I am tired of being a man . . .

Just these opening lines made me ecstatic. I never read anything so wonderfully zany before. I loved the wild imag-

Written for a symposium on Neruda's influence in *Quarry West*, 1988.

ery, the romantic posturings, the flowery, exaggerated rhetoric. What people reading Marquez's *One Hundred Years of Solitude* later on called "magic realism" was already to be found in Neruda. Here was a freedom of the imagination that was completely absent in the American poetry I was seeing in the journals of the day. All those dreadfully lifeless and boring imitations of Eliot and seventeenth-century poetry, which I, like so many of my contemporaries, was trying in turn to imitate, since I didn't know any better. I didn't know about the Beats or the Black Mountain poets, because their work was hard to find in Chicago where I was growing up. I had read some French Surrealism and knew about modern art and its various manifestos, but Neruda and the other South Americans were a complete surprise.

Years later, when I rediscovered some of the poems I wrote in that period from 1958 to 1961, I was amused and a little embarrassed by how much they were influenced by Neruda. I had, of course, subsequently found more translations of his poetry. There was H. R. Hays's *Twelve Spanish Poets*. There was Robert Bly's magazine *The Fifties*. *The Elementary Odes* was published by Cypress Press in a translation by Carlos Lozano. And there were also Ben Bellit's translations.

"Ode to a Pair of Socks," or the "Ode to an Onion"—I must have read those poems hundreds of times. It's a poetry that makes me happy. I want to go out and live life to the fullest, eat an enormous meal, drink wine with friends, stay up all night long, and then for breakfast make a big tomato salad with onions, basil, and green peppers from the garden.

Neruda is the poet of the senses. In poem after poem he celebrates that wonderful moment when we feel intensely alive and full of love for everything existing. He is gregarious, and he has the generosity of spirit that, perhaps, only Whitman before him had to that extent. He gives us the hope that a poetry can be written that anyone who loves life can understand.

That was the ideal as far as I was concerned: to write a poem that people who don't read poetry would appreciate but that my pompous literary friends and my professors would not. I found in Neruda a way to be joyfully subversive, to be funny and serious at the same time. He cured me of the excessively intellectual approach to poetry with which I was imbued. Years later, I used to read his poems to students in gang-ridden New York public schools, and had my proof. The tougher the crowd, the more they enjoyed the poems. When I read the same poems in prep schools, the students were confused. They didn't know why Neruda was writing about such unimportant things.

I forgot what year it was when I heard Neruda himself read at the Y in New York. The house was packed. He read in Spanish and several of his American translators read the English versions. I knew the poems so well that I could even follow them with my elementary Spanish. He read, and I wept. I sat there with tears streaming down my face, which made my wife laugh. I was very moved. In addition to the poems themselves, there was the beauty of the Spanish language in the mouth of a great poet. What more can one ask of life and art?

Wonderful Words, Silent Truth

Every object is a mirror . . .

—They're not really object poems.
—What are they then?
—They are premonitions.
—About what?
—About the absolute otherness of the object.
—So, it's the absolute you've been thinking of?
—Of course.

Form is the visible side of content. The way in which the content becomes manifest. Form: time turning into space and space turning into time simultaneously.

I admire Claude Levi Strauss's observation that all art is essentially reduction and Gertrude Stein's saying that poetry is vocabulary.

Chance as a tool with which to break up one's habitual associations. Once they're broken, use one of the pieces to launch yourself into the unknown.

We name one thing and then another. That's how time enters poetry. Space, on the other hand, comes into being through the attention we pay to each word. The more intense our attention, the more space, and there's a lot of space inside words.

From notebooks, 1975–85.

Connotations have their non-Euclidean geometries.

A song sung while understanding each word—the way Billie Holiday or Bessie Smith did it.

Vitrac called chance a "lyric force." He's absolutely right. There's a kind of dreamy exhilaration in not knowing where one is going.

Seeing with eyes open and seeing with eyes closed. That's what Elizabeth Bishop's poem "Fish" is about.

For imagination, inside every object there's another object hidden. The object inside is completely unlike the outside object, or the object inside is identical to the outside object, only more perfect. It all depends on one's metaphysics, or rather, whether one leans toward imagination or reason. The truth probably is that the outside and the inside are both identical and different.

My complaint about Surrealism: it worships imagination through the intellect.

—Form thinks, not the content.
—What the hell does that mean?
—But, if form is time and time thinks . . .

The poem I want to write is impossible. A stone that floats.

Duncan's profound words: "The mysteries of here and there, above and below, / now and then, demand new / figures of me."

Avant-gardism: seeing the history of art and literature as "progressing," the future being superior to the past, etc. For literary conservatives it's the other way around. There was once a Golden Age, and so on. We are just dwarfs on the back of giants, etc., etc.

Some twentieth-century intellectual types: those who welcome the philosophical contradictions, those who ignore them, and those who despair because of them.

Form is not a "shape" but an "image," the way in which my inwardness seeks visibility.

Artaud: "No image satisfies me unless it is at the same time knowledge."

My ambition is to corner the reader and make him or her imagine and think differently.

The time of the poem is the time of expectation. I believe some Russian Formalist said something like that.

I'd like to show readers that the most familiar things that surround them are unintelligible.

There is a weather report in almost every folk poem. The sun is shining; it was snowing; the wind was blowing. . . . The folk poet knows that it's wise to immediately establish the connection between the personal and the cosmic.

Poetry is a way of knowledge, but most poetry tells us what we already know.

Between the truth that is heard and the truth that is seen, I prefer the silent truth of the seen.

If I make everything at the same time a joke and a serious matter, it's because I honor the eternal conflict between life and art, the absolute and the relative, the brain and the belly, etc. . . . No philosophy is good enough to overcome a toothache . . . that sort of thing.

Thought in art is customarily confused with didacticism, with paraphrasable content, with "message." Thought in genuine art is always none of these things.

Contradictory pulls when it comes to making a poem: to leave things as they are or to reimagine them; to represent or to reenact; to submit or to assert; artifice or nature, and so on. Like the cow the poet should have more than one stomach.

There are three kinds of poets: those who write without thinking, those who think while writing, and those who think before writing.

Awe (as in Dickinson) is the beginning of metaphysics. The awe at the multiplicity of things and awe at their suspected unity.

To make something that doesn't yet exist, but which after its creation would look as if it had always existed.

The never-suspected, the always-awaited, the immediately recognized new poem. It's like Christ's Second Coming.

The poet is a tea leaf reader of his own metaphors: I see a dark stranger, a voyage, a reversal of fortune, etc. You might as well get a storefront and buy some Gypsy robes and earrings! Call yourself Madame Olga.

"What do poets really want?" I was asked that once by a clever professor of philosophy. It was late at night and we were drinking a lot of wine, so I just said the first thing that came into my mind: "They want to know about things that cannot be put into words."

An object is an encyclopedia of archetypes. I've learned that writing "The Broom."

Ambiguity is the world's condition. Poetry flirts with ambiguity. As a "picture of reality" it is truer than any other. Ambiguity is. This doesn't mean you're supposed to write poems no one understands.

Metaphor offers the opportunity for my inwardness to connect itself with the world out there. All things are related, and that knowledge resides in my unconscious.

The poets and writers I admire stood alone. Philosophy, too, is always alone. Poetry and philosophy make slow solitary readers.

God died and we were left with Emerson. Some are still milking Emerson's cow, but there are problems with that milk.

A recent critic has enumerated what he calls "the lexicon" of recent poetry. The words mentioned as occurring repeatedly are: wings, stones, silence, breath, snow, blood, water, light, bones, roots, jewels, glass, absence, sleep, darkness. The accusation is that the words are used as mere ornaments. It doesn't occur to the critic that these words could have an intense life for a mind with an imaginative and even a philosophical bent.

The worst offense one can commit in a poem is humor. Irony and wit are acceptable, but laughter in a lyric poem is a serious transgression. Great art, or so people think, is serious business. The more solemn the tone, the worthier of respect it is. Plato censored poetry that provokes "frivolous laughter," and so do my students reading Frank O'Hara.

Imagism is realism minus the moral. If Imagist poems were didactic, people would find them more acceptable.

Here's the moralist definition of "the beautiful": Not life as it is, but life as it ought to be.

What John Gardner in his *Moral Fiction* doesn't get is that the history of Western literature is really a long quarrel between the poet and the priest, the poet and the schoolteacher.

How to communicate consciousness . . . the present moment lived intensely that language locked in the temporal order of the sentence cannot reproduce?

Time is the lapse between perception and recognition (consciousness of that perception).

The last hundred years of literary history have proved that there are a number of contradictory and yet, nevertheless, successful ways of writing a poem. What do Whitman, Dickinson, Baudelaire, Rimbaud, Yeats, Williams, and Stevens have in common? Plenty, and nothing at all.

Poem: a theater in which one is the auditorium, the stage, the sets, the actors, the author, the public, the critic. All at once!

Myth: finding a hidden plot in a metaphor. There's a story and a cosmology in every great metaphor.

I love the saying "No two eggs are alike."

There are critics unable to experience the figurative, the way some people are color blind and tone deaf, or lack a sense of humor. They can tell it's a metaphor, but it doesn't do anything for them. If it cannot be paraphrased, this then becomes a further proof that it's completely worthless.

Metaphor proves the existences of Heaven and Hell.

Ideological criticism is always stationary. It has its "true position," from which it doesn't budge. It's like insisting that all paintings should be viewed from a distance of ten feet and only ten feet. Many paintings do not fully exist at that distance, of course. Besides, one is never at a single vantage point except intellectually. In life and in art, one is simultaneously in several places at once.

It is the object I'm watching, the fork, for example, which sets up the rules of its visibility.

The modern poem implies a modern aesthetics and philosophy. Poetry written in that mode cannot be understood without an understanding of modern intellectual history. This seems pretty obvious, but not to everyone. Many of our leading literary critics have not read as widely as our poets. The poets' readings are much more adventurous. And then, of course, there's painting and cinema, which the critics customarily forget.

It goes without saying that a Chinese has a greater appreciation of Chinese poetry than a Westerner. But poetry is not only what stays in the cultural context, but what transcends it.

The theory of archetypes: inside is where we meet everyone else; it's on the outside that we are truly alone.

Two ways of creating: to uncover what is already there or to make something entirely new. My problem is that I believe in both.

"Momentary deities" is, I believe, how the Greeks thought of words.

Consciousness: separating "I" from "it." The "I" can be spoken but not the "it."

"He has great images," we used to say, and we meant that the poet kept surprising us by his wild associations. Total freedom of the imagination was our ideal then. That's all we loved and demanded from the poetry we were going to write.

Beautiful, mysterious images are static. Too many such images clog the poem. A mysterious image is a holy, wonder-working icon. How many of those can you have in a single poem?

The inventor of the modern metaphor, Arthur Rimbaud, regarded himself as a seer. He saw that the secret ambition of a radical metaphor is metaphysical. It could open new worlds. It could touch the absolute. He gave up poetry when he began to doubt that truth.

Most poets do not understand their own metaphors.

I proclaim the hermeneutics of the perfectly clear. Its ambition is to find hidden opacities in the brightest sunlight.

Nietzsche: "A small overstrained animal whose days are numbered" proposes the "object of its love." That's what my poems are about.

Contemporary poets have for the most part forgotten about symbolism, especially its one great insight that Being cannot be stated but only hinted at.

It's curious that there are still critics who equate imagination and fantasy.

Certain philosophers have understood the poetic image better than literary critics. Bachelard, Heidegger, and Ricoeur come to mind. They grasped its epistomological and metaphysical ambition. The critics too often see the image solely in literary terms.

What a mess! I believe in images as vehicles of transcendence, but I don't believe in God!

Heisenberg's "uncertainty principle" has comic potential, besides being the best formulation of the comic spirit.

"We understand others as a result of the speed with which we pass over words," says Valéry. This describes for me what happens in a free verse poem. One speeds up, or one slows down the flow of words. One pauses. . . . One says nothing. . . . Then, one resumes one's pace.

The common object is the sphinx, whose riddle the contemplative poet must solve.

J. Riddel: "What is it the poet reaches? Not mere knowledge. He obtains entrance into the relationship of word and thing."

Beware of synchronicity—"the meaningful coincidence of an external event with an inner motive." That way madness lies.

The provincialism of our criticism: One reads B and Y, but not Z, D, or N. One has an extremely narrow knowledge of the field, yet nevertheless likes to generalize about American poetry.

"The Triumph of Pere Ubu," an essay on History and Stupidity. That would be something!

"Truth eludes the methodical man," says Gadamer. Thank God! That's why poets have a chance.

Poe: "The word infinity, like the words God and spirit, is by no means the expression of an idea, but an effort at one."

What to call "It"? You need a word. You need several words for the ineffable.

Here's what I understand to be the spirit of Dada: Gentle, kind, most indulgent and benevolent reader, friend of friends, brother and sister of my soul, kiss my ass!

Form is "timing"—the exact amount of silence necessary between words and images to make them meaningful. The stand-up comedians know all about that.

Poe in *Eureka:* "Space and duration are one." Space is the image of Time in the moment of consciousness.

The fate of the poet is the fate of the soul in every man and woman.

I always had the clearest sense that a lot of people out there would have killed me if given an opportunity. It's a long list. Stalin, Hitler, Mao are on it, of course. And that's only our century! The Catholic Church, the Puritans, the Moslems, etc., etc. I represent what has always been joyfully exterminated.

Note to future historians: Don't read old issues of the *New York Times*. Read the poets.

Time is the subjective *par excellence*. Objectively, time doesn't exist, despite the appearances. This is Gurdjieff's idea, which fascinated my father.

Imagism is about the passion for accuracy. To get it right, etc. But, it's not easy to get "it" right! A philosophical problem. Imagism is the epistemology of modern poetry.

A metaphysics without a self and without a God! Is that what you want Simic?

"The iron hand of necessity shaking the dicebox of chance." I believe that's Nietzsche's phrase. I've been worrying about it for years.

The most profound thing that Emerson said about the poet is that he knows the Secret of the World: that Being passes into Appearance, and Unity into Variety.

I have an idea for a new game of chess in which the value of each figure would change from move to move. Pawns could become knights, the king could turn into a queen, and so on. The choice would be the player's. His opponent would have to anticipate all the additional options. A game of infinite and dizzying complexity.

A poem is a place where affinities are discovered. Poetry is a way of thinking through affinities.

The cookie-cutter poets. The cookie-cutters are made of gold and sit under glass in their grandparents' parlors.

I like the folksy vulgarity of Chaucer, Rabelais, and Cervantes.

There are poets who treat you like an imbecile, and there are poets who treat you like a poet.

"The greatest danger to the poem is the poetic." I don't remember who said that.

What the political right and left have in common is their hatred of modern art and literature. Come to think of it, all the churches hate it, too, which doesn't leave us many supporters. On the one hand we have the dopey rich who collect Andy Warhol's soup cans, and on the other hand some poor kid in love with the poems of Russell Edson and Sylvia Plath. Oh boy!

Everything was right with the world until that yokel Rimbaud opened his mouth.

To the narrative poets: What do you think Pound meant when he said "Do not retell in mediocre verse what has already been done in good prose"?

Everybody wants to be able to paraphrase the content of the poem, except the poet.

The encounter between philosophy and poetry, my little lambs, is not a tragedy but a sublime comedy.

Thomas Campion

He was both poet and musician. The musicians have praised his music and the poets his poetry. Pound and Eliot called him one of the finest lyric poets in the English language. If one defines the lyric as a poem to be sung, he was a master of it. He brought music and poetry together and made us believe they are sister arts, and Orpheus their first great practitioner.

He lived in what was certainly the golden age of these two distinct art forms. Born in 1567, Campion was a contemporary of Shakespeare, Drayton, Marlowe, Nashe, and Jonson in literature, and Byrd, Morley, Gibbons, and Dowland in music. "A man of faire parts and good reputation," wrote Samuel Daniel, even while attacking Campion's essay on prosody. There were many such testimonials of his worth during his lifetime.

Ben Jonson is an exception. He knew Campion but offered no praise. Is it possible that the author of "To Celia" was tone-deaf? Jonson complained that "Buchanan [Campion's tutor] had corrupted his ears when young, and learned him to sing verses when he should have read them." That's the view that prevailed. We no longer sing our poems; we read them to ourselves, and rarely aloud.

Campion wrote airs for solo voice, songs accompanied by a lute. One note to a syllable is how one sets words to music in such a song. The melodies are simple, and the words come across distinctly. "Air," of course, implies lightness, airiness. Campion did not care for richness of musical texture. It ob-

Written as an introduction to *The Essential Campion* (New York: Ecco Press, 1988).

scured the text. The same is true of fancy metaphors and conceits. They could not be sung with a straight face.

Today we have recordings of Campion's songs and can hear what he was after. There was a time, however, a period of almost two hundred years, when even his poems were not available. They lay buried in Elizabethan songbooks: that kind of singing had long gone out of fashion. The great Romantic poets never heard of Campion. Even Shelley, who compared the poet's psyche to an aeolian lyre, knew him not. Campion was not rediscovered until the late nineteenth century. Since then, it's been difficult to imagine the history of English poetry without him. Whoever still dreams of a poem in which language begins to resemble music must take him into consideration.

Campion's first songs were published in 1601. They appeared in a *Book of Ayres* by one Philip Rosseter, Lutanist. These were not his first published poems. He was known previously among his contemporaries as a Latin poet, and had in fact already written a great deal of poetry in that language before turning to songwriting.

It's no wonder that he knew Latin poets. He attended Peterhouse College, Cambridge, where classical literature was studied seriously. The students rose between four and five in the morning for prayers and were expected to study till late into the evening. Poor Campion didn't even get to go home on vacation. He was an orphan. His father had died when he was nine, and his mother, who had remarried, shortly after. His stepfather and guardian didn't care to see him very often. At Peterhouse, appropriately, like all the other students, he was advised to avoid "finery" and wear "sad colours."

We can assume that Campion participated in the intellectual life of the place. He was, by all accounts, a friendly sort, a man who always had a large circle of friends. His college fostered the study of medicine, and the university itself was famous for its degrees in literary study and music. What we do know is that he left without obtaining a degree, some say because he was a Roman Catholic and Catholics were not permitted to receive one.

Whatever the case may be, we find him next at Gray's Inn

in 1586, there, presumably, to study law in the footsteps of his father, who was a minor law clerk at Chancery Court when he died. Nothing came of it. He participated in masques and revels, which were part of the social activity of the inns of the royal court, and he wrote poetry in Latin. There was obviously a literary circle there, young men showing each other poems and discussing literature.

We know nothing, on the other hand, of Campion's musical education. In 1589 the first book of Italian madrigals appeared in England, Nicholas Young's *Musica Transalpina*. It is well known that at the inns there were many fine musicians and singers. Both the lute song and the madrigal were at the height of their popularity. Campion's interest was both typical of his time and somewhat unusual among those who were poets. He had a single-minded devotion to the lute song.

Campion supported himself during these years on the small inheritance his mother had left him. After the money ran out, he found himself nearing forty and without a profession. In 1602, he enrolled as a medical student at the University of Caen in Normandy, a medical school popular with English students for being close to home, and for giving quick degrees. Campion got his after only three years of study. For the rest of his life he practiced medicine.

The evidence suggests that he was a good doctor and that his reputation among his colleagues was considerable, although he held a degree not recognized by the Royal College of Physicians. The practice did not make him rich. Campion died in 1620 with twenty-two pounds to his name. The money went to his friend and collaborator, Philip Rosseter, so we can assume that he had no close family left.

Campion published quite a bit during his lifetime. In addition to the poems in Latin (*Poemata*, 1594) and the first book of airs, we have his important *Observations in the Art of English Poesie* in 1602, *Two Bookes of Ayres* in 1613(?), *The Third and Fourth Booke of Ayres"* in 1617(?), several masques, an essay on musical theory, and a final volume of new and revised Latin epigrams, brought out the year before he died.

"What epigrams are in Poetry, the same are Ayres in musicke," Campion wrote. He made early connection between the two. "Their perfection comes from being short and well-seasoned," he added. His own poems have the terseness, the wit and bite, of a finely wrought epigram.

In *Observations in the Art of English Poesie,* Campion argued for the superiority of classical prosody over English practice. He preferred the way the Latin poet measured the length of the syllables to the native poet's reliance on stress alone. He understood the difficulty of applying Latin prosody to "our toonge," and asked that closer attention be paid to syllable length so that the measure might be more precise.

The underlying concern here is, obviously, the art of setting words to music. He says: "In joyning words to harmony there is nothing more offensive to the eare than to place a long sillable with a short note, or short sillable with a long note, though in the last the vowell often beares it out." His other complaint is rhyme—that "Medieval barbarism" he calls it! The attention it receives comes at the expense of the integrity of the individual line of poetry. Campion gives examples of rhyme used to conceal the defects of the line. For him the line is all important. As Robert Creeley says, "The line is the means to focus, is that which says 'how' we are to weight 'things' we are told. And as it is there, to do this work, so the words break through their *sense*"—and into their song, Campion might have added. "What musick can there be where there's no proportion observed?" he writes. "The eare is a rational sense and a chief judge of proportion." As the musician fine-tunes his instrument, so the poet fine-tunes the lines of his poem.

Leibniz said that "the unconscious mathematical operations of the soul are the basis of our enjoyment of music," and Campion would have agreed. This is the deepest belief of the lyric poet. "All inmost things are melodious," said Carlyle. Music is the way in which the solitary self relates to something beyond itself, "the bridge between consciousness and the unthinking sentient or even insentient universe," in Pound's words.

In Campion's view, "The world is made by Simmetry and proportion, and is in that respect compared to Musick, and Musick to Poetry." The cosmology of the lute song is Pythagorean. As above so below. "Tune thy music to the heart," our poet says.

Economy of expression is both an ideal and a practical necessity for Campion. His is a poetry of little ornamentation, minimum imagery: pithy as the epigram. Adjectives are avoided and so are lengthy descriptions. On the other hand, there are many conventional poetic phrases, many well-worn Petrarchan echoings. The subject and the manner is almost always familiar; all invention is concentrated on variation and the departure from convention.

Surprisingly, Campion's poems, despite their literary context, have something of the folk song about them. In both, understatement is the rule, what is known in rhetoric as paralipsis: the suggestion by the deliberately concise treatment of a topic that much of significance is being omitted, while, nevertheless, it is being implied. This is especially true of Campion's later poems, in which the psychology of the speaker begins to play a greater role. He or she may say one thing, but we know there's more to the story.

The subject matter of his poems is the tragicomedy of courtship, marriage, adultery, sexuality—in other words, the eternal human predicament: subjects and situations that are cliché-ridden but that also contain eternal truths. Campion has been called "platonically cold," but in my own view he's really a tough-minded realist.

If there's one theme that seems to run through most of the poems, it is that of seduction. "Born of literature, able to speak only with the help of worn codes" (Barthes), the act itself and its tragicomedy is entirely a matter of language. Campion's lovers yearn to fall under the spell of words, but somehow they're unable to. They're constantly eavesdropping on themselves. The sublime-turning-into-the-ridiculous is their lot.

If ever poetry needed to be read aloud, his ought to be. With him, the phrase "auditory imagination" begins to acquire meaning. The ancients used to make a distinction between truth that is seen and truth that is heard. Every great lyric poem recapitulates the whole history of inspired listening to the mother tongue.

Ivan V. Lalić

> ... when they forever become
> Enigmas to each other, and elude each
> Other's grasp, they who lived in common
> Memory of him, and when sand
> And willows are blown away, and temples
> Are destroyed, when the honor
> Of the demigod and his disciples
> Is scattered to the winds and even
> The Almighty averts
> His face, leaving nothing
> Immortal to be seen in the sky ...
> —Hölderlin

> We define poetry as an unofficial view of being.
> —Wallace Stevens

Ivan V. Lalić, who published his first book of poems in 1955, belongs to a generation of Yugoslav poets who thought of themselves as Modernists in the early years after the Second World War. It was a period dominated by literary and political battles over socialist realism. That struggle was fundamental then, and continues to be so in Eastern Europe. The so-called Realists believed that literature must, first of all, serve society, that society is governed by immutable Marxist laws, and that any deviation from the straightforward, socially tinged depiction of reality is a manifestation of bourgeois formalism and aestheticism. The Modernists refuted these views as undemocratic, constrictive, and unfaithful to the spirit of Marxism. They demanded the abolition of dictates by the authorities, a

---

Introduction to *Roll Call of Mirrors: Selected Poems of Ivan V. Lalić* (Middletown, Conn.: Wesleyan University Press, 1988).

greater freedom of creativity, and, above all, the freedom to experiment. A number of the older Modernists were Surrealists before the war and their sympathies were still with the international avant-garde and its program. The battle, when all is said and done, was essentially between literary conservatives and poets who wanted a new kind of poetry.

Even these terms are not very useful when one comes to Lalić's poetry. Regarded as a Modernist, committed as much as they were to a renewal of tradition—a renewal rather than a break—his poetry has always seemed less modern than that of his contemporaries. The spirit of his poetry is classical. There are not many poets since Hölderlin who feel as deeply the Greek literary and philosophic tradition. Cavafy is certainly another poet who lives in that world, but he is interested more in history than in myth. In the context of postwar Yugoslav poetry, Lalić's "modernism" really comes down to his lifelong commitment to what he regards as the oldest and the most genuine poetic tradition available to a poet writing in his part of the world.

This is what Lalić himself says in an essay: "In contemporary poetry as in contemporary experience of the world, certain accents come easier when one says no to the world, when one sings revolt, disagreement, the cracked vision, the disharmony." In a recent interview he affirms "that he never could or wanted to sing negation." Being a modern poet for him is a far more complex issue. "Is there a poem of the present moment?" he asks. "Only in the context of the total vision of Time," he replies.

His eleven collections of poetry make clear how seriously he regards such matters. History and mythology are present in his poetry from the very beginning. He is not interested in just retelling the old stories; he meditates on them. Perhaps all stories are about time, all poems about the timeless moment? The experience of Time in all its dimensions is certainly at the heart of Lalić's lyricism.

Classical Greek poetry and the great Romantic visionary poems are his models, but his work is not derivative. Lalić has too good an eye for the world he lives in, and a superb ear for the spoken idiom. The mastery of his free verse and his diction is that it retains the memory of the traditional meters and rhetoric without ever sounding archaic. If the task of the poet is to "purify the language of the tribe," as Mallarmé said, Lalić shows that this can be done through the words the tribe uses every day.

Ezra Pound knew that. Lalić knows that he did. He has translated most major American and English poets of the last hundred years. This includes most of Whitman and a lot of Dickinson. He has done the same with French poetry. He has also translated the work of Hölderlin, the one poet who had, without doubt, the greatest influence on him. All this has been of utmost importance for his own work. Lalić's mastery comes, I believe, from understanding profoundly the range of options a poet writing today has. He told me once in a letter: "I guess if I wrote in English I would try to learn some things from Stevens. Impossible to *follow* him, of course (the way one can follow, let's say, Pound), but one can profit a lot."

There's another way in which his work as a translator has been important. Translation is the closest possible reading one can give a poem—a lover's reading. Translation is also a type of shamanism. One reads words and sees images inside somebody else's head. Then one speaks in tongues. In the end, all poetry is translation of an uncertain and often absent original.

The contemporary American poet Charles Wright puts it this way: "Poetry is an exile's art. Anyone who writes it seriously writes from an exile's point of view." This makes sense in relationship to what Lalić is doing. We are all exiled from our origins, his poems seem to tell us. We all have our Byzantium from which we have been cast off, to which we belong. There's the historical Byzantium, which was the spiritual and the intellectual center for Serbs and other Southern Slavs, and there's the mythical one of Yeats. Lalić's is neither exclusively one nor the other. In his poetry the historical and the mythical are in dialogue. They converse in images and metaphors. The obsessive subject of Lalić's poetry is a search for origins, and Byzantium is one of its names.

In introducing his poetry, I once wrote the following: "It is his attempt to establish contact with a complex ancestry that has always been there, a dream, a magnificent poetic image lying dormant in the unconscious, a kind of Atlantis of the inner world of his people. I am not referring here to literary tradition but to something much more basic, a need to keep certain channels to the past open. As Lalić says: 'The poem lives in a forgotten place.' This is the labor that contemporary Serbian poetry simply had to undertake in order to become more deeply conscious of its own identity and in Lalić's words: 'piece its homeland together.' What I like about this undertaking is the drama of the two parallel levels: that of history and recurrence and that of the individual occurring uniquely. . . . The hope for him, as for all of us, is to reach understanding of a unity that exists between the myth and his own life. . . . The buried flame of the myth illuminates the present moment. What comes out of this understanding is the poem turned not nostalgically toward the past, but becoming a sign in which the future can be read."

Two of Lalić's most recent collections have interesting titles. One is called, in English, *Interference on the Line,* and the other *Passionate Measure.* They tell us a great deal of what goes on in the poems: the old connection no longer works. There are other voices on the line. We have trouble getting through to our origins. Poetry can be thought of as a "passionate measure" measuring the distance to our origins. In Heidegger's words: "To write poetry is measure-taking, understood in the strict sense of the word, by which man first receives the measure for the breath of his being." It is the experience of that distance, that nearness which gives the poet the poem.

In an interview Lalić quotes his friend the critic Zoran Mišić, to whom the elegy "Rovinj Quartet" in [*Roll Call of Mirrors*] is dedicated, who says: "The poet no longer goes from myth toward poetry, but from poetry toward myth." This strikes me as being absolutely true of the practice of some of the best modern poets. What needs to be asked is: How does one go toward myth? And the answer is, I think, that one goes by image and metaphor. Metaphor gives access to myth. It initiates the poet into the mystery of analogy. All things are related. "The mystery of here and there, above and below, now and then, demand new figures of me," says Robert

Duncan. The poet searches for identity among all the differences the world offers by the way of metaphor.

Lalić understands that analogy is a cognitive tool. Only analogy can rediscover the world and recover its numinous presence. Every poet makes a decision as to what is authentic. In Lalić's poetry, metaphor is that truth.

Before metaphors, however, come images. The world first exists in its infinite particulars. The world is. The poet cannot say what . . . only what it is like. Thinking in poetry is a dangerous game with mirrors. To find resemblance is to find how images reflect each other.

I say a dangerous game because the true work of art works. The poem is working out the poet's fate. Ours, too, if he happens to be a great poet, and Lalić certainly is one.

It has been almost twenty-five years since I first read and translated Lalić. I found a few of his poems in an anthology of contemporary Yugoslav poetry, liked them immediately, and wanted to see what they would sound like in English. I suppose this is the most common reason people turn to translation. One wants to share one's pleasure with others who do not read the language. A friend I showed Lalić's poems to said they remind him of Rilke's. Everybody loved his strange and beautiful images. I published these early versions in the undergraduate literary magazine, *Washington Square Review*, published at New York University, I believe in 1965.

The poems came from the cycle of love sonnets to Melisa, with which I was to have a twenty-year obsession. Twenty-two sonnets out of the total of thirty-one are included in this book. Translating them, I discovered what I was to rediscover many times afterward, and that is the complexity of Lalić's imaginative structures and word-play. His intellect dances between words; one keeps discovering, seemingly forever, new nuances and subtleties. It takes a long time to get one of these poems right, but the labor is full of rewards, as it can only be when one comes to realize what makes a work of art what it is.

My next translations were done in the late 1960s. I met the poet and publisher Bill Truesdale, who, as it turned out, was in the process of putting together a selection of Lalić's poems. He had met the poet the previous year while Lalić was traveling in the United States, and out of that meeting their collaboration began. Lalić provided literal English versions, which Truesdale turned into poetry. I was asked to participate in the project, which I did, by bringing my own few translations and by checking the ones they did. The book was published in 1970 by New Rivers Press and was called *Fire Gardens*. It was well received.

I think it was during the time we were working on that book that Lalić and I started corresponding. (We didn't actually meet till 1972.) What astonished me, both from his letters and from meeting him face to face, is his superb knowledge of English. Not only did he know the literature, but he had a deep appreciation of its idioms. When it came time for him to check my translations, I had someone who understood what problems I was encountering and could offer help.

What I finally translated over the years, and what I am including in this book, are poems of his that I admire and that seem to work well in translation. There were, of course, many others of which I thought highly in the original, but which I was unable, for one reason or another, to render properly.

My method as a translator is to stick to the literal whenever possible. That works up to a point. Beyond that, as everybody knows, no two languages share an identical associative context. Cultural and historical experiences differ. Behind an idiom there might be lurking views of man, gods, earth, heaven, which the native speaker intuits. The translator has to be "the poet of poetry," as Lalić himself has said, to convey all that is unspoken and of supreme importance in the original.

I am mainly thinking of lyricism. Lyricism is neither feeling, nor occasion, nor thought about the occasion. It is more than that. It is the awe at the way the words sound and sing in the language one is writing in. Lalić himself says: "For me listening ordinarily comes before what I could call naming, or recognizing. . . ." He has also told how he composes his poems in his head for years before he puts them down on paper. "For the longest time—before it comes to be said, that is, spoken— the poet's work is only listening," says Heidegger, and this might be true also of the translator. The translator, like the poet, listens to the unspoken.

The whole issue of translation is especially interesting to me because I have—so to speak—two mother tongues. Serbian is the first language I spoke, but I have known and used, almost exclusively, the English language for thirty-five years. So, there are two mothers, or just one mother speaking from different corners of her mouth like some wonder-working Byzantine icon. That's the translator's ideal. Perhaps no such identity is ever possible between two languages—or if it is, then, like poetry itself, it is already in the realm of the miraculous.

Serbian Heroic Ballads

I

I was ten years old when I first read these heroic ballads. It was during one of the bleak postwar winters in Yugoslavia. There was not much to eat and little money to heat our apartment properly. I went to bed as soon as I got home from school, to keep warm. Then I would listen to the radio and read. Among the books my father left was a thick anthology of *Serbian Folk Poems*. That's what they were called. In the next few years I read the whole volume and some of the poems in it at least a dozen times. Even today I can still recite passages from my favorite ballads. None of this, of course, was in any way unusual. Every Serbian loves these poems.

The Kosovo Cycle I learned to appreciate somewhat later. I first fell in love with the ballads that describe the adventures and heroic feats of various rebels during the Turkish occupation. They are "action packed," as they used to say on movie posters. The Turks are the cruel conquerors and the Serbs are either clever slaves or outlaws.

In the ballad "Little Radojica," for example, the inmates of Aga Bećir Aga's notorious prison are rejoicing because their pal, little Radojica, still hasn't been caught. But then, he is. They throw him in the deepest dungeon among the now despairing prisoners and he figures out what to do. He tells his

---

Preface to *The Battle of Kosovo* (Athens: Swallow Press/Ohio University Press, 1988).

comrades to inform the Aga as soon as the day breaks that he died during the night. That's what they do. The Turks carry Radojica, who is pretending to be dead, into the prison yard. The Aga takes one look and tells his servants to throw the stinking corpse into the sea. But now his wife and daughter show up. The wife says that Radojica is only pretending, that they should build a fire on his chest to see if he stirs. They do, and he doesn't. Then she asks them to hammer nails under his fingernails. Still Radojica doesn't budge. The Aga has had enough, but the wife has one more idea. She asks her daughter to dance with her girlfriends around the dead man, and the daughter, we are told, is very pretty. There follows a wonderful description of the daughter's flowing robes and jingling bracelets as she dances. Poor Radojica is opening one eye and his mouth is curling up into a grin. The daughter sees this and throws her veil over his face. Radojica is finally thrown into the sea where he manages to swim out to a far rock to nurse his wounds and wait for the night to come. The Aga is having supper with his family when Radojica breaks in, kills the parents, frees the prisoners, and takes the daughter to be his wife.

I hope the bare plot outline of "Little Radojica" conveys how entertaining these poems are. What is missing, of course, is the building suspense, the wonderful descriptive details, as well as the humor and poetry of the piece. Even in these later ballads the complexity of the vision, for which the Kosovo Cycle is famous, is present. It's not that Turks are all bad and the Serbs all heroes. The view of history and the appraisals of the individual figures found in the poems are full of ambivalence and psychological savvy. These rebels are often ordinary brigands out to enrich themselves. They collaborate with the enemy and seem to have every ordinary human weakness. If they're heroes, it's in spite of themselves. Neither the tribe nor the hero is idealized. The world view of these poems is different from that of those in the Kosovo Cycle, where the mythic and epic dimensions reign supreme. Nevertheless, both touch the earth. A sense of proportion and a sense of realism is what they share.

II

One day in school, in what must have been my fifth or sixth grade, they announced that a *guslar* would perform for us. This was unexpected. Most city people in those days had never heard a *gusle* being played, and as for us kids, brought up as we were on American popular music, the prospect meant next to nothing. In any case, at the appointed time we were herded into the gym where an old peasant, sitting stiffly in a chair and holding a one-stringed instrument, awaited us. When we had quieted down, he started to play the *gusle*.

I still remember my astonishment at what I heard. I suppose I expected the old instrument to sound beautiful, the singing to be inspiring as our history books told us was the case. *Gusle*, however, can hardly be heard in a large room. The sound of that one string is faint, rasping, screechy, tentative. The chanting that goes with it is toneless, monotonous, and unrelieved by vocal flourishes of any kind. The singer simply doesn't show off. There's nothing to do but pay close attention to the words, which the *guslar* enunciates with great emphasis and clarity. We heard "The Death of the Mother of the Jugovići" that day and a couple of others. After a while, the poem and the archaic, otherwordly sounding instrument began to get to me and everybody else. Our anonymous ancestor poet knew what he was doing. This stubborn drone combined with the sublime lyricism of the poem touched the rawest spot in our psyche. The old wounds were reopened.

The early modernist Serbian poet and critic, Stanislav Vinaver, says that the sound of *gusle* is the sound of defeat. That, of course, is what the poems in the Kosovo Cycle are all about. Serbs are possibly unique among peoples in that in their national epic poetry they celebrate defeat. Other people sing of the triumphs of their conquering heroes while the Serbs sing of the tragic sense of life. In the eyes of the universe, the poems tell us, the most cherished tribal ambitions are nothing. Even the idea of statehood is tragic. Poor Turks, the poet is suggesting, look what's in store for them.

Vinaver also speaks of "heroic spite." Achilles rebelled against all the Greek chieftans; Gilgamesh against the gods.

The poet of the Kosovo Cycle rebels against the very idea of historical triumph. Defeat, he appears to be saying, is wiser than victory. The great antiheroes of these poems experience a moment of tragic consciousness. They see the alternatives with all their moral implications. They are free to make a fateful choice. They make it with full understanding of its consequences.

For the folk poet of these poems, true nobility and heroism comes from the consciousness of the difficult choice. They say the old Greeks had a hand in this. Very possibly. The world from which these poems came didn't change that much from the days of the Greek dramatists.

There's also the Christian context, but even that doesn't fully explain the poems' view of the human condition. The Serbs do not think of themselves as Christian martyrs, or as chosen people with a mystical destiny. The ballads are remarkable for their feel for actual history. The mythical is present but so is realism. This is the fate of all the small peoples in history and of all the individuals who find themselves the tragic agents and victims of its dialectics.

III

Everyone in the West who has known these poems has proclaimed them to be literature of the highest order that ought to be better known. And, of course, there have been many translations since the mid-nineteenth century. Except for one or two recent exceptions, they do not resemble the originals at all. We either get Victorian Homer or just plain incompetence.

There's no question that the poems are hard to translate. Their literary idiom is somewhat unfamiliar. There's nothing quite like it in English or other western European literatures. One has to invent equivalents rather than to just recreate familiar models.

Perhaps the main stumbling block is prosody. The ten-syllable line in Serbian is a mighty force. Each syllable is audible and distinct. The trochaic beat sets a fairly regular and steady pace. The translator immediately runs into a problem.

The lines in English translation tend to be much longer. Both the conciseness and the syllabic quality of the verse are lost. One is left with a lot of words per line and no meter to recreate the narrative drive of the original.

Then there's the problem of the diction. The early translations tend to poeticize and idealize what is really a model of economy and understatement. This is not Ossian, or even Tennyson. In the Kosovo Cycle there's an absolute minimum of verbosity and epic posturing.

What John Matthias and Vladeta Vučković have done strikes me as an ideal solution. Breaking the line at the caesuras gives it a lilt, an anticipation at the break, a "variable foot" effect in the manner of William Carlos Williams's later poetry, that captures the pace of the narrative. Matthias is a superb craftsman. His intuition as to where and how to adjust the tempo of the various parts of the poem to achieve a maximum narrative and dramatic result almost never fails him. He grasps the poetic strategies of the anonymous Serbian poet as much as Pound did those of Chinese poetry.

The other great accomplishment of these translations is in the language. When it comes to fate and tragedy, the original seems to be telling us, use only absolutely necessary words. The clarity, the narrative inevitability, and the eloquence of the poetry of the Kosovo Cycle come through in these translations. I don't know any better ones. If the Serbian heroic ballads are indeed great poetry, as people keep saying, you will get a taste of that greatness here.

Introduction to the Poetry
of Aleksandar Ristović

> In the back of the nunnery
> there's a small outhouse
> with a half-open door and evening visitors.
> While one is inside,
> another waits her turn
> with her nose in the book.
> And while the first one exits,
> straightening the robes,
> her face almost radiant,
> the other one steps in,
> peeks into the spotless hole,
> trembling with terror
> that what lies at the bottom
> may leap into her face
> and leave a mark on her flushed cheek
> in the shape of a devil's cross.
> ("Monastic Outhouse")

At times one comes across a poet who strikes one as being absolutely original. There's something genuinely different about him or her, a something that one has never quite encountered in all the poets one has read before. "I will never look at the world in quite the same way," one realizes at once, and that's what happens. From that day on, one feels deeply and fatefully changed by the experience of that reading.

The poetry of Aleksandar Ristović had that effect on me.

Introduction to *Some Other Wine and Light,* selected poems of Aleksandar Ristović (Washington, D.C.: Charioteer Press, 1989).

When I first read his poems in Belgrade in 1982, I was astonished. "Who is this man?" I kept asking everybody, meaning really, how did he come to write the way he did? Nobody could tell me. The Yugoslavs I showed his poems to were as puzzled as I was. Even though Ristović has published fifteen books of poetry and has received two major literary prizes, he is not very well known, since he has never belonged to any official or unofficial literary movement. "He's not seen much in public," someone told me. "He lives a quiet life," someone else explained. The little I know about him comes from what he told me in a letter and from what I have read on the jackets of his books, and it's not much.

Ristović was born in 1933 in Čačak, a fairly large town some hundred miles south of Belgrade. After receiving a degree in literature from the University of Belgrade, for many years he taught Serbian language and literature on the elementary and high school level in his hometown. In recent years, he has worked as an editor of children's books for a large Belgrade publisher. In addition to his volumes of poetry, he has published a novel, a book of translations of French poetry, and some literary criticism.

His biography, as is often the case, doesn't explain his poetry. What is obvious in reading Ristović is that he has intimate knowledge of a certain kind of small town life, its people and its manners. There's something medieval about his poems. They remind me of old woodcuts illustrating proverbs, the dangers and delights of the Seven Deadly Sins. What these artists of long ago have in common with Ristović is a love of the grotesque and the unexpected juxtaposition. Men and gods, heaven and earth, the sacred and the profane, and everything in between are part of their vision. It's all fatefully connected, tragically and comically mixed up. A stew, as it were, of angel and beast cooked up by the hardest of realists.

"No ideas but in things," said William Carlos Williams, and many poets, including Ristović, would have to agree. The difference between poets comes down to how they experience the commonplace realities of their everyday life. Whatever ideas they may eventually have come out of such unpremeditated particulars. The poet who loves the wind has different gods than the poet who loves the stones in the earth. What we make passionately ours is what defines us. The possessions of even the greatest poets are small. A few objects, a few vivid scenes and shadowy figures—and that's all. What may look like poverty to everybody else, represents, potentially, great riches to the poet.

All great poetry is the contemplation of a few essential images—essential to the poet first, that is. Ristović knows all about that. He has his butchers, his pigs, his tailors, and a few other recurring figures. What runs through the poems is an astonishment and fascination with human folly. The poet pleads with his characters, questions them, warns them, though they cannot hear him. He's like the insomniac who talks back to the TV screen. It's a silent film without subtitles. The images move very slowly and keep returning like an old, half-forgotten dream. In most of Ristović's poems, time has stopped and is waiting for someone to catch up with it.

I'm moved, and I think other readers will be too, by Ristović's compassion. There's a great deal of human suffering in these poems. There's Good and Evil. They walk the earth. Good is weak, doing a few small kindnesses, providing a few moments of beauty. Evil is mighty and cruel and unseeing. Here's a twentieth-century poet who believes in the Devil. The Devil is ever-present, not so much as a separate being, but as a part of ourselves liable to leap out at any moment. Like the nun who reads the prayer book while waiting her turn at the door of the monastic outhouse and worries about the Devil at the bottom of the hole, we too are all precariously balanced between the spiritual, the physical, and that unnameable something, that X that is a part of any life-equation.

It is not just in the works of such painters as Vermeer and El Greco that light plays such a mystical role. In poetry, too, there's light, the light of vision. One doesn't always know its source. It illuminates in the old sense of "enlightening," of making known what till now was veiled in darkness. Perhaps such light exists nowhere in nature, and what we are seeing in these painters, and in such poets as Ristović, is the glow of their inwardness, the very same light that makes their dreams visible at night. Otherwise, how is one to account for the great psychic weight and mystery these works of art possess?

Finally, to imagine another's existence with such intensity, as Ristović does in these poems, is a religious experience. Imagination and love, the commingling of matter and spirit, flesh and soul, and the two forms of time, eternity and the present moment. These are all elements of great poetry, and, as my old friend the poet Frank Samperi used to say, "all great poetry is religious poetry."

Art Hodes

Late at night one should go where blues is played. Let it be cold, too. Some Tuesday in January with a few snowflakes along the dark avenues and treacherous-looking sidestreets. It's good to be alone then, or if there's a friend along, let him or her not say much. It's too late for trumpets, trombones, and drumrolls. What one needs after midnight is a piano, the master working alone, the few solitary lovers of the art slouched over their drinks in sweet anticipation. The whole city is asleep. All the upright citizens are in bed. There is just us and the blues.

I heard Art Hodes on a night like that in a place called Hanratty's in New York City back in 1981. I knew the man's music well. One of the scratchiest records in my collection is of Hodes romping with Sidney Bechet on "Weary Blues." One of my all-time favorite jazz piano pieces is Hodes's version of Hoagy Carmichael's "Washboard Blues," on an album appropriately called *Art for Art's Sake*. The art Hodes practices is now rarely heard. There's a blues-piano tradition going back to the early twenties, at least, which includes such greats as Jelly Roll Morton, Leroy Carr, Jimmy Yancey, and many other lesser-known figures like Walter Rolland, Walter Davis, Cripple Clarence Lofton, and Little Brother Montgomery.

This tradition is separate from that of the stride piano as practiced by James P. Johnson, Fats Waller, or Art Tatum. For one thing, it's less technically dazzling, more succinct, more single-minded, as it were: a minimum of notes, a lot of feeling, and a disarming melodic directness with its roots in coun-

First published in the *Missouri Review* in 1987.

try blues and gospel. It's the music for insomniacs, the philosophers of a single dark thought. Pascal was a blues artist, and so was Sappho. The music, the night I heard Hodes, was wordless, but language was never far off. Listening to him is like overhearing a man making a poem, saying the words to himself, cancelling one phrase, adding another.

I've heard a number of great piano players play the blues but not one as poignantly as Hodes. The night my brother and I arrived at Hanratty's, he was between sets. We got the table right next to the piano and looked around. Hodes was seventy-seven at the time, balding and a bit bent, but otherwise robust-looking. He was born in Nikoliev, Russia, and with his big nose is the spitting image of my Russian father-in-law. What amazed me about him, what delighted me about all the jazz musicians I've seen, is the knowledge that these people work at night. Sixty years of playing into the wee hours while the century turned on its mad roller coaster. A labor of true love, surely, since there was never any money in it, and certainly no social prestige. The music was first played in dives, whorehouses, after-hours dancehalls for an audience of blacks and a few whites. Most of the early white jazz musicians were sons of immigrants, or, like Hodes and Joe Venuti, born in the old country. No doubt about it, the people who played this music were considered the scum of the earth.

In any case, Hodes finally took his seat at the piano. Silence, and then those first few, lovely, still exploratory notes of a slow, slow blues. "This is the real thing," it struck me. This is what this man knows how to do well, and it comes from the depths of his being.

"Save It Pretty Mama," might have been the tune, or his own solemn "Selection from the Gutter." We heard both that night. Sitting so close to the keyboard, I observed the economy of the playing. So few notes and such a powerful effect; a meditation with just a hint of swing underneath. This is the art of nuances, stops, accents, allusions, summoning our musical memories and other memories of moments such as this one. The piano player is all attention and so are we. Clarity reigns. Lacking a bass and a drum, Hodes kept time with flicks of his left wrist, pausing, advancing, making us hear Time, or rather making a design out of Time.

It's not easy to convey the complex associations such well-played blues evokes. As someone said, writing about music is like singing about architecture. There were tears in my eyes because of the sheer beauty of the playing.

Blues is sad, of course, but there's no slobbering in it, no self-pity. Cosmic solitude, certainly, but with a sly, comic touch. The blues lyrics are tough. There's genuine self-knowledge in them and wit. They have a merciless discernment of the human condition. They know about men and women. They know about sexuality. In comparison, socialist realism is just sentimental crap, and so is so much other literature. I admire the laid-back quality of the blues, the understatements and omissions that tell everything. The point is you can tell a story in a few notes, in a few words. There's much here for an American poet to learn from.

We wanted Hodes to play all night. The few of us remaining, that is. We applauded; we cheered. He acknowledged our enthusiasm with a bow and a grin, and said, "I'm an old man who ought to be in bed." Then he played a few more numbers for us.

Notes on Bata Mihailovitch's Paintings

Wittgenstein: "Don't think, look."
de Kooning: "Don't look, paint."

Bloodied landscapes. The way the earth must look to the crows who are bringing evil tidings in Serbian folk ballads.

This is the sky the saints saw at the height of their visions. Heretics, too. A sky like a burst of admiration. A sky that makes one silent.

The heavens on the eve of a great battle to which soothsayers were summoned to interpret the omens. "Bloody flags moved from east to west," says some ballad.

At times, too, one saw the long faces of the elders of our tribe peeking out of the clouds.

Tottering architectures of the spirit. Works vast in scope partially abandoned. Scaffoldings on air. Ruins.

Historical hurricanes sweeping up the cities, churches, and their saints. Images out of wonder-working icons roaming the sky. The clouds are full of them. When it rains in Bata's paintings, holy relics fall.

The dark night of the soul. Phantoms of the Serbian Historical Opera. Vampires. Ancestral ghosts. Memory the abbreviator. Memory and its shadow theater.

Bata Mihailovitch, born in 1922, is one of the best Yugoslav painters. This note was written for an exhibition of his paintings in Beograd, Yugoslavia, in May, 1989.

Untitled (1985)

My grandmother knew how to cast with her hands the shadows of St. George and the Dragon on the kitchen wall. She made us children tremble.

And always tragedy! Martyrdom! Suffering! Tragic heroes struggling like flies in the soup of history.

The gods do not play, as some say. They cook and stir the thick soup. I can see the green stuff floating, but there is also plenty of red meat in the pot.

Every genuine imagination has a history, and it has a geography, which is to say that nobody owns the imagination. We are locked in one of its zoo cages. (It has many.) The sign says the cage contains a family of Balkan monsters. You've heard about the ancient Greek artists, supposedly, using as models the inner visions they had of their gods? That's what I'm talking about.

On the other hand, I ask you, what true artist isn't both the inheritor and the repudiator of his ancestry? There's Bata and anti-Bata. These canvases are their heroic battlefields.

I think of his painting as the sum of all his contradictions. A great clutter, yes! But, everything in order too. Is that possible? Of course.

What I admire in Bata is the constant play of opposites. The abstract, the representational, the sacred, the profane: the angels ascending to heaven, but also the dancing bear brought to the fair by the gypsies.

Here's how my old friend Percy Knight used to explain it after a few drinks: "The problem with most painters," he'd say, "is that they either paint the Madonna or the peasant peeing into a bush." What Percy liked about someone like Bosch, for example, is that when he painted one, he always remembered the other and made sure they're side by side in the same picture.

I call Bata's space inner space. Self-lit, inhabited, oneric space? The hole where one crawls in to hide oneself? Is that what we see in so many of his paintings? The dark, crumpled bedding where he keeps tossing and turning.

Painting like poetry is an aspiration toward a new image of the world. Bata . . . the fire-thief. His fundamental faith in transgression. If any painting is metaphysics, this is it!

"I laugh at metaphysics . . . which devours me," says Gombrowitz.

Is Bata a religious painter? (Critics often talk of his debt to Byzantine art, etc.) Here's the answer: "Malevich once pointed out that in the work of a famous medieval icon painter the hairs of God's beard were exactly the same as the hairs on the devil's tail."

Painting like Bata's preserves the fabulous. It's as busy as Arabian nights. I suppose Mondrian had his own linear, religio-geometric version of plenitude. Think of "Broadway Boogie Woogie"! The problem is that Mondrian is an intellectual absolutist. His paintings end up resembling those utopian models of harmonious societies which, as everybody knows, turned out to be penitentiaries in real life.

I like the story Vasari tells of how Piero di Cosimo sat plunged in contemplation of a wall upon which people passing used to spit. Out of these random stains he formed battles, fantastic towns, and most magnificent landscapes.

Modern painting is like the Balkans. Its wisdom is that of a sheep who sucks several mothers.

I feel great kinship with Bata and his vision. We find ourselves in a similar intellectual predicament. We are neither exiles nor do we belong anywhere in particular. Men on the rubbish heap of history, as Marxists would say. How wonderful! An ideal place to be as far as I'm concerned. The junk of the Old and the New World all around us.

Hans Hofman: "Art is a reflection of the spirit, a result of introspection, which finds expression in the nature of the art medium." Ergo, painting is soul-making. Five fingers marching on the road to Calvary when they're not dipping that devil's tail into a bucket of paint.

I'm not convinced that psychic turmoil is the ultimate subject of a work of art. I like what Harold Rosenberg has to say about this: "The arrangement of colors and forms on the canvas never encompasses completely the experience that moved the artist to execute it, and the painted surface is always in some respect nothing more than a hint."

Guston: "What you see is not what you see."

In painting as in poetry there's something that eludes any theory, any attempt to name it. (Thank God!) The density of Bata's imagery, the richness of his allusions, is the result of a passionate engagement with the history of painting and its possibilities, but then something else happens. That "something" is what makes us say later that we can always recognize one of his paintings.

I watched Bata paint a few times. It looked to me as if he was putting things in their right place, things he didn't know existed just a moment before. And he kept erasing! He erased as much as he painted. I understood then and there his admirable capacity to surprise himself, to innovate, to break his old habits and make painting an adventure. Every day going into the unknown to find another image of himself and all of us existing.

William Stafford's
"At the Bomb Testing Site"

At noon in the desert a panting lizard
waited for history, its elbows tense,
watching the curve of a particular road
as if something might happen.

It was looking at something farther off
than people could see, an important scene
acted in stone for little selves
at the flute-end of consequence.

There was just a continent without much on it,
under a sky that never cared less.
Ready for a change, the elbows waited.
The hands gripped hard on the desert.

A political poem in which not a single political statement is
made, what Stafford himself calls more "nonapparently politi-
cal than apparently political."

Let me quote Nietzsche here: "The consequence of reverie
which would borrow from intelligence the means to force
upon the world its folly. . . . We are a race committed to the
test of the act, hence pledged to the bloodiest fate."

Written for a *Field* magazine symposium on the poetry of William
Stafford and published in 1989.

In poetry a choice is made about the part that will represent the whole. Form, in its deepest sense, is selection. True form is the product of an extraordinary vision.

There's a lizard at the bomb testing site. The poem is an attempt to measure everything according to the duration and intensity of that little life.

A "weasel-worded" poem.

The naked world. The innocent lizard. A most primitive form of life. Ugly. Expendable—like those laboratory animals stuck inside a maze under the bright lights.

One assumes they're afraid too.

"How pure and great must be the cause for which so much blood is spilled," says Aleksandar Wat.

For now, just the timeless moment. Just the lizard, the desert. He's panting, trembling a little.
Think of Elizabeth Bishop's "Armadillo," the fire raining on him . . . That will come later.

History is marching . . . or, History is a throw of the dice . . .

The poem is an attempt to convey certain old premonitions. The first lizard knew the world would end some day.

And at the heart of it—incomprehension! Bewilderment!

Out there, perhaps, scratched in stone, there's the matchstick figure of the Indian humpbacked flute player. He is surrounded by other matchstick figures. They are enacting a scene, a sacred dance . . .

The sphinx is watching. An American sphinx waiting for history. The hands grip hard, so we are on the very verge. It is the instant in which all past and all future wait suspended.

One should speak of Stafford's disappearing acts. As in "Traveling through the Dark," he leaves us at most crucial moments. At the end of his great poems we are always alone, their fateful acts and consequences now our own to consider.

Solitude as an absolute, the only one.

The heavens above couldn't care less.

The poet asks the philosopher in us to consider the world in its baffling presence.

An American sphinx in the desert of our spirit. Let us keep asking her questions.

In the meantime, we can say with Heidegger that poems such as this one open the largest view of the earth, sky, mortals, and their true and false gods.

UNDER DISCUSSION
Donald Hall, General Editor

Volumes in the Under Discussion series collect reviews and essays about individual poets. The series is concerned with contemporary American and English poets about whom the consensus has not yet been formed and the final vote has not been taken. Titles in the series include:

Forthcoming volumes will examine the work of Langston Hughes, Philip Levine, Muriel Rukeyser, H.D., and Denise Levertov, among others.

Please write for further information on available editions and current prices.

Ann Arbor   **The University of Michigan Press**